COPYRIGHT

GW00514894

LIMITATION OF LIABILITY

<u>Introduction To Word Processing</u>

Before working through this *Word Processing* resource pack, it is important that you read the following information that has been written to offer you guidance on how to get the best out of this resource pack.

The resource pack has been divided into units. Each unit consists of a number of IT-related categories. Throughout these categories are tasks, designed to help you understand how to use the computer and how the different parts of the computer work.

At your own pace, you are required to read and work through the resource pack.

The introduction section of this resource pack is mainly theory-based, but it is essential that you read through this section and understand each category. Some parts of the workbook will be considered recap for those who have completed the Word Processing resource pack 1.

At key moments throughout the resource pack, you will be instructed to perform a practical assignment or task. These tasks are there to demonstrate, with a practical hands-on approach, the important theoretical aspects of the computer that might otherwise be difficult to understand by merely reading through the resource pack.

It is important that you carefully read through each category before attempting to do the tasks, as this will equip you with the knowledge you will need to answer the questions contained within each task.

Don't worry if, occasionally, you find yourself having to refer back to the section you have just read in order to complete a task. Only through reading each category and completing the accompanying tasks will you correctly learn about the principles of word processing.

Consolidation exercises are also contained within each resource pack. These exercises provide a further opportunity to recap the various categories and tasks that you will have previously undertaken, whilst working through the resource pack.

By following these simple instructions and correctly using this resource pack, you will find that learning about word processing will be far more enjoyable and so much easier.

Contents

©Tektra TEKWP2RP1102

On completion of this introduction, you will have learnt about:

- **Word Processing**

- **Planning And Preparing Common Types Of Document**

  - Checking Data Availability

- **Paper Sizes And Orientation**

  - Paper Sizes
  - Paper Orientation

- **Envelopes**

Word Processing

Word processing is the most popular computer application and the one which most people are familiar with. It is the entering, manipulation and presentation of text.

Text can be moved around and errors corrected easily. Different styles and sizes of text can be adopted and layout can be amended without difficulty. Spelling and grammar can be checked as you go along or after completing a document. Word processing also allows for the integration of charts, spreadsheets and pictures within your work.

Because of the high level of facilities to prepare professional looking documents, word processors have largely replaced typewriters in the business world.

Word is one of today's most popular Windows-based word processing systems. You have everything you need within the application to create anything from a simple document of a few lines long to a highly professional 500 page report.

Common Types of Document

Using a word processing package such as Microsoft Word 2000 allows you to produce many types of documents for use in the home or business environment. The documents can either be created from a blank document or by using one of the built in 'templates' or 'wizards' within the package.

Templates

Every Microsoft Word document is based on a template. A template determines the basic structure for a document and contains document settings such as fonts, page layout, special formatting and styles. The two basic types of templates are global templates and document templates. Global templates, including the Normal template, contain settings that are available to all documents. Document templates, such as the memo or fax templates, contain settings that are available only to documents based on that template. For example, if you create a memo using the memo template, the memo will use the preset fonts and styles etc, letting you add your required text. Word provides a variety of document templates or you can create your own document templates.

Wizards

A 'wizard' is a special kind of template. When you use a basic template, you input the text and formatting into the template. However, when you activate a 'wizard' to use a template, it will display a series of questions about the document you are about to create such as:

What style would you like?
Do you want to include a title?
Which header items would you like to include?

When the series of wizard questions have been answered, your template document will appear in the Word window. This can either be saved and printed or edited further if required. Wizards are a fast and easy way to create documents.

All available templates and wizards can be found by clicking on **File**, **New** from the menu bar in Word 2000 (Fig 1). This will display the **New** dialogue box. Templates and Wizards can be identified by their icons.

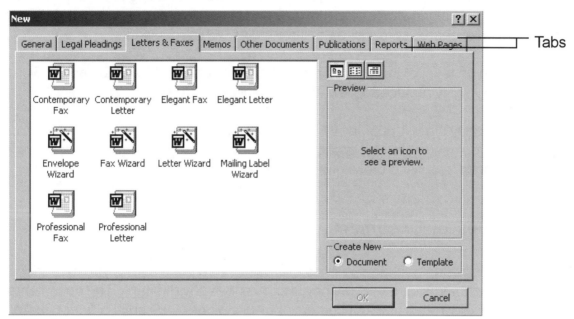

Fig 1

 Template icon   **Wizard icon**

Types of document are grouped into categories and can be viewed by clicking on the 'tabs' in the **New** dialogue box. Categories include:

General - This includes a blank document (based on the normal template), a web page and an e-mail message.

Legal Pleadings - A pleading wizard.

Letters & Faxes - This category includes a mixture of templates and wizards to produce letters and fax cover sheets. There are different designs available. Also included are envelope and mailing label wizards. This section has all that is required for creating a letter or fax ready to send.

Memos - This category includes a mixture of templates and wizards for use in creating memoranda.

Other Documents - This category is used for creating miscellaneous documents such as an agenda, a calendar or a resumé.

Publications - Create brochures, manuals, directories or theses using this category.

Reports - This category offers three designs for reports.

Web Pages - Create web pages using this category. You can either select a design from those available or use the web page wizard.

Planning And Preparing Common Types Of Document

Before using the computer to produce a document, it may be necessary to plan a draft layout. This can be achieved by producing a preliminary sketch on paper.

The sketch should not include the actual text to be typed into the document as this would defeat the object of using a computer! However, reference is made to the criteria as listed below:

Type of document	(Blank document or existing template or wizard)
Page orientation	(Landscape or portrait)
Paper size	(A4 or A5 etc)
Font and font sizes	(is there a company standard?)
Logo	(is this existing or needs to be created?)
Objects	(such as an image, Clip Art or chart)
Overall layout	(with regard to sections, columns, margins, text positioning etc)
Text emphasis	(bold, underline etc)

The example below shows sketch criteria to take into consideration when planning and producing a company newsletter:

Newsletter

Portrait orientation; A4 size; Arial font throughout, suitably sized

Company logo to be inserted at the bottom left

Risk Results Chart to be inserted in the third column

Overall layout - 3 equal columns, with main heading 'Outsource Newsletter' in a section of its own at the top of the document.

See Fig 2 for an example of the sketch produced.

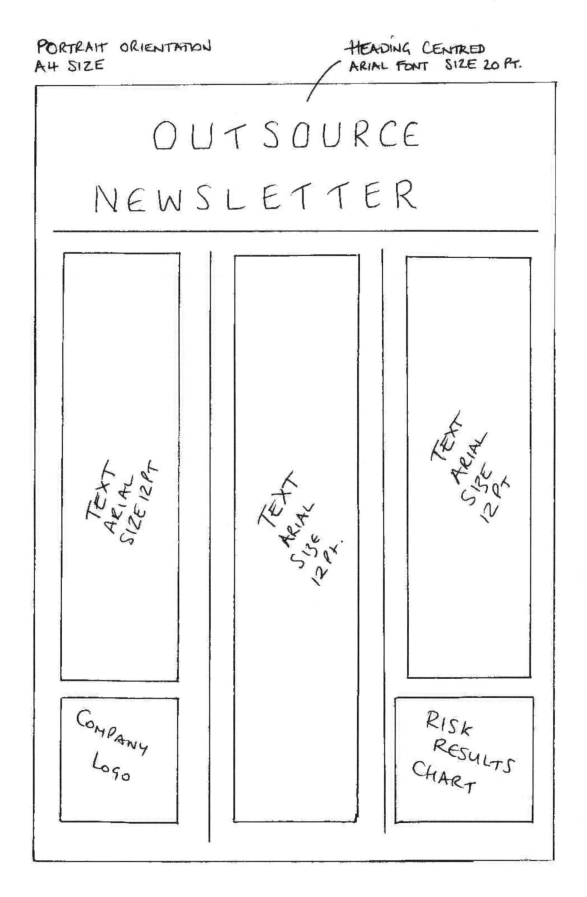

Fig 2

Common types of document include letters, faxes, memoranda and reports. These documents are all included as templates in Microsoft Word 2000.

This workbook will help you learn about creating common types of documents, together with adding features to enhance the document's layout, style and structure.

Adding attributes to text such as bold or underlining will ensure some sections stand out from others. This is useful when including headings in your document.

The layout of documents should be as comprehensive as possible, ie spacing text appropriately. Text should not appear cluttered or squashed. Paragraphs on a page should be evenly spaced and formatted consistently.

This workbook will guide you through inserting objects into documents such as images and charts and other Word documents. When planning the production of the document, ensure this data is available.

T A S K

1. *Plan the production of a flyer (leaflet) for your company:* **Outsource Ltd**. *This will be used to advertise a workshop which is available to all staff. The flyer must include the date on which the workshop will be held and the time.*

   A preliminary sketch is required for the flyer, which will be produced on the computer at a later date. Produce a sketch taking into account the criteria below:

Document type:	*Flyer (leaflet)*
Page orientation:	*Portrait*
Paper size:	*A4*
Font and font size:	*Arial (adjust font sizes to suit)*
Logo:	*Outsource logo*
Objects:	*Suitable image (cartoon type)*
Overall layout:	*The workshop name should be in large text to stand out in the top half of the page.*

   All other workshop information to be placed in the bottom half of the page accordingly.

   Include text colour where appropriate.

   Margins should be set to 3cm all around.

2. *Keep the sketch to hand.*

Checking Data Availability

Flyers and brochures are useful documents for promoting and marketing a business. Careful use of text, graphics and numerical data can enhance the appearance of the flyer. However, the availability of this type of material should be checked when producing the draft layout.

For example:

You have been asked to create a flyer for a company which is to include the company logo (which includes a graphical image) and a chart/graph (which contains the profit details for the company). Is this information available?

The information may be contained in another file, on another computer or in another office location. Other considerations to take into account would be:

The format of the data, ie is it saved in electronic form?
If photographs are required, what form are they in?

In addition to the above, the standard draft layout considerations should also be taken into account.

Document type	Used for	Layouts	Page orientation
Letter	Communicating between people and businesses. Usually sent via post.	Usually A4 or letter-sized paper. May have a printed header containing the name of a company or person.	Portrait
Facsimile	Communicating between people and businesses and usually sent via a facsimile machine.	Usually A4-sized containing a printed header section stating who the fax is from and the date and subject. It may also contain how many pages are being sent.	Portrait
Memorandum	Communicating between people and businesses. Usually sent manually, by hand or by post.	May be A5 or A4 in size. May or may not contain a header. Usual headings include to, from, date, cc and subject.	Portrait or landscape
Minutes	A document used to record events at a meeting. Usually distributed by internal mail or post. May be sent electronically.	Usually A4 in size. Contains information such as the company name, the location, date and time of meeting.	Usually portrait, but may be landscape

Document type	Used for	Layouts	Page orientation
Report	May be a short or lengthy document reporting on any given subject. Usually has an introduction, a main body and a conclusion and summary. May be sent via post or electronically.	Usually A4. The author's name or company name may appear on the report.	Usually portrait
Invoice	A form used for billing another for services or goods. Usually sent via post, but may be sent electronically.	Company name, address and possibly telephone number details, who the invoice is made out to and the invoice number. Details of the billing amount and services/goods. Usually A4, but may be A5 if a small company.	Usually portrait, but can be landscape
Agenda	A document used to inform others on the topics of a meeting that is to be held. Usually distributed via internal mail or post. May be sent electronically.	Usually A4, but this may depend on the number of items. Gives information such as the date and time of the meeting and attendees. Also lists the topics to be discussed.	Usually portrait, but may be landscape
Resumé or curriculum vitae	A document used to hold personal details on an individual. This is usually sent with a job application.	Usually A4 in size, contains the person's name, address, DOB, schools attended, qualifications, professional qualifications, previous and present employment and other skills.	Portrait
Electronic mail	A message document that is typed on screen using special software. Used to communicate quickly between people using the Internet. Similar to a memorandum, but electronic.	As this is on screen, the layout may not be applicable. However, if printed, may be produced on A4 paper.	If printed, usually portrait

Paper Sizes And Orientation

Paper Sizes

Easily the most identifiable paper size would have to be A4, as it is the standard UK size for letters and business documents. The document that you are currently reading is almost certainly A4 in size. The measurements for portrait A4 (portrait being a sheet of paper that is standing upright or vertical) are:

21 centimetres (cm) across by 29.7 centimetres (cm) down
or
8.16 inches across by 11.69 inches down

Figs 3 and 4 illustrate a variety of paper sizes with the measurements given in centimetres. Dimensions for paper sizes are normally given with the width measurement first.

A6	**10.5 x 14.85**
A5	**14.85 x 21**
A4	**21 x 29.7**
A3	**29.7 x 42**
A2	**42 x 59.4**

Fig 3

Fig 4

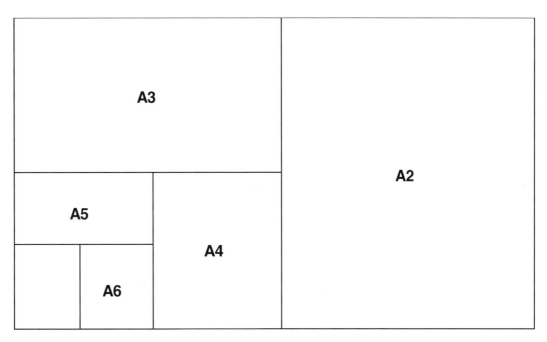

<u>Paper Orientation</u>

There are two types of paper orientation, **portrait** and **landscape**. Portrait has the short edge of the paper appearing at the top (see Fig 5). Landscape has the long edge of the paper appearing at the top (see Fig 6).

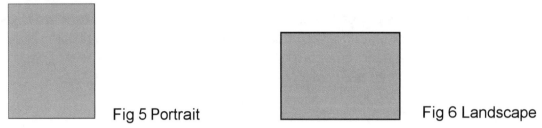

Fig 5 Portrait

Fig 6 Landscape

Envelopes

Envelopes come in a variety of sizes, just as the items to be sent through the post can also vary tremendously. The UK standard-sized envelope, measuring 21.9 centimetres wide by 11 centimetres high, is used for sending A4 (the standard UK paper size). Figs 7 and 8 show dimensions for the three most commonly used envelope sizes.

Fig 7

Standard UK Envelope	**21.9 cm x 11cm**
A5 Envelope	**22.8 cm x 16cm**
A4 Envelope	**32.3 cm x 22.9 cm**

Fig 8

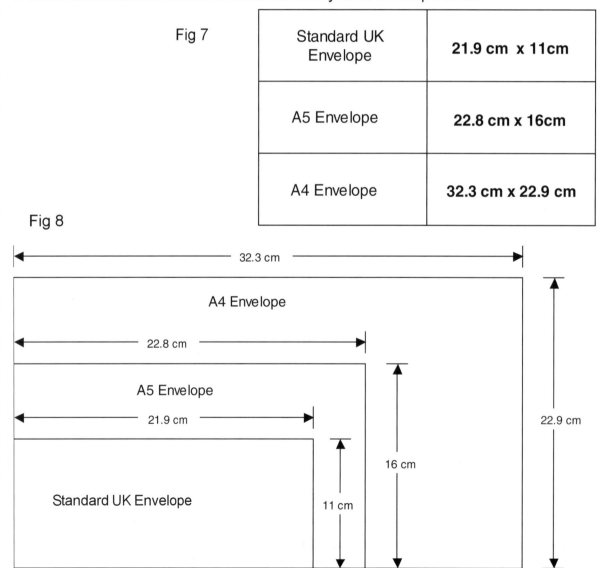

**T
A
S
K**

Scenario

You work for a company that manufactures furniture. They require a new range of stationery, including an invoice, a letterhead, a fax header and a memorandum. You are required to produce a range of drafts, using the correct paper orientation and sizes. This should be indicated on the sketch. Also indicate all alignment, fonts and font sizes as required.

The company information is as follows:

Fix It Designs Limited
1020 The Strand
Carpingham
London
CP45 8HY

Tel: 09786 395996
Fax: 09786 395997

Web address: www.fixitdesigns.co.uk

Email address: fixitdesigns@madeup.com

1.   *Produce a draft layout of the invoice. If required, obtain an example of a real invoice and use this as a template on which to base your draft.*

2.   *Produce a draft layout of the letterheaded paper. Again, use an example if one is available.*

3.   *Produce a draft layout of the fax header. Again, use an example if one is available.*

4.   *Produce a draft layout of the memorandum. Again, use an example if one is available.*

5.   *Note down on each draft why you chose the orientation and paper size.*

Word has an excellent facility to enable you to produce envelopes and labels using a computer. However, this is only a valuable feature if your printer is capable of printing onto envelopes!

You can create an envelope or label by activating the dialogue box when in a new blank document and typing in the address required or you can open the corresponding letter and select the address to send to.

In the example (right) the address to be displayed on the envelope has been highlighted (selected) and the **Envelopes and Labels** dialogue box activated by clicking on **Tools**, **Envelopes and Labels**.

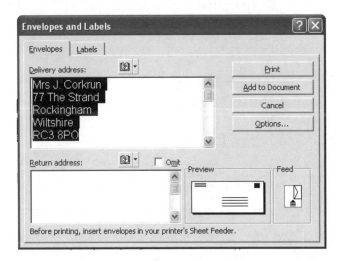

Notice that the highlighted address has been carried forward into the dialogue box on which to base the Envelope options and the **Envelopes** tab is automatically selected.

Provided your envelope has been correctly loaded into the printer you can directly print from here by clicking on the **Print** button. If you are not sure that you have the correct size envelope selected, use the **Options** button and select the correct type.

Envelopes usually state the size code on their box or packet and this may correspond to the list of envelope sizes stored within this dialogue box. It is worth checking for the correct size before printing to save making mistakes and wasting envelopes. You could even make a practise print on a plain piece of paper first to ensure this is the correct size.

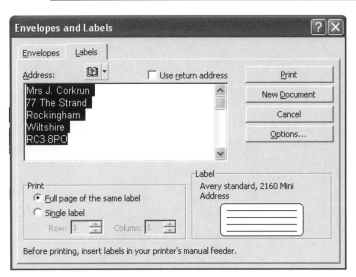

To print labels, select the **Labels** tab.

Again, you can print straight away if the labels are loaded and ready in the printer.

However, it is essential that you have the correct label size selected.

Labels come in standard sizes and if you have purchased your labels from a reputable stationer, the size should be displayed on the box or packet and this will correspond with the size in the **Options** dialogue box in the **Labels** section.

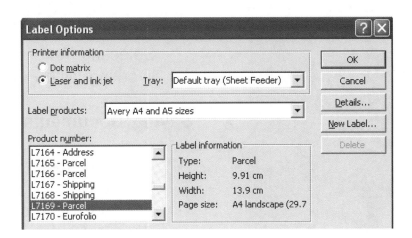

You can also choose to print a full page of the same label or a single label in the **Print** section of this dialogue box.

T A S K	1.	*Produce a mock envelope using the address from the draft layouts (Fix It). Select a Size 11 envelope. Print the envelope on plain paper.*
	2.	*Produce a mock page of labels using the address from the draft layouts (Fix It). Select a full page of the same label and size - choose **Avery A4 and A5 sizes** and product number **L7169**. Print the labels on plain paper.*

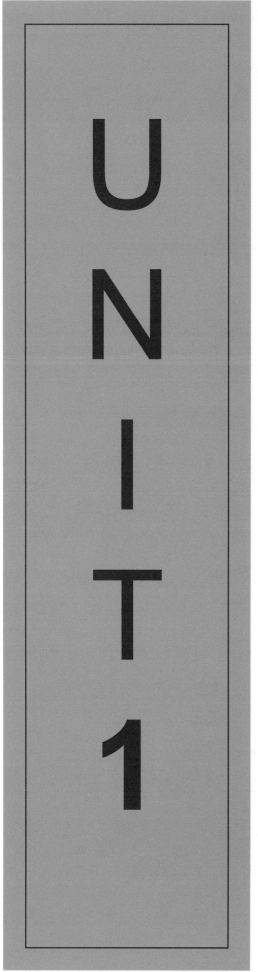

On completion of this unit, you will have learnt about and practised the following:

- **Word Processing Recap**

  - Opening The Word Processing Application

- **Creating And Opening New Documents**

  - Creating A New Document
  - Inserting Text Into A New Document
  - Selecting Text
  - Working With Paragraphs

- **Saving Documents**

  - Saving A Document To A Floppy Disk
  - Saving A Document To The Hard Disk
  - Saving A Document To A New Folder

- **Closing Documents**

  - Closing A Word Document
  - Closing Microsoft Word 2000

- **Opening Existing Documents**

  - Opening An Existing Document
  - Switching Between Open Documents

- **Creating A Back Up Copy**

Word Processing Recap

Opening The Word Processing Application

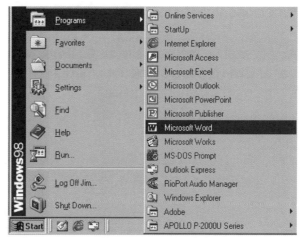

To open Microsoft Word 2000, click

Start, **Programs**, **Microsoft Word**

Alternatively, click on the Microsoft Word icon on the Desktop.

T A S K

1.   *Start Microsoft Word 2000.*

The application will open, together with a new blank document.

The application name is displayed here and the new document will be assigned a temporary file name.

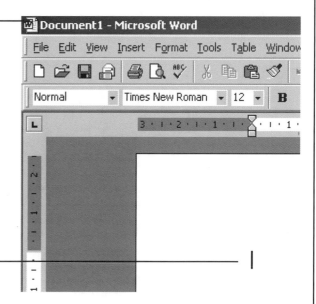

The 'cursor' flashes in the work area of the window. This indicates that the new document is ready to receive your text.

Creating And Opening New Documents

Creating A New Document

When opening Microsoft Word 2000, it will automatically open a new blank document.

An alternative method is to select **File**, **New** (Fig 9) from the menu
bar or **Ctrl+N** (for a blank document). This will enable you to select
the type of document required.

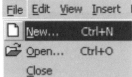

Fig 9

The **New** dialogue box will then appear (Fig 10).

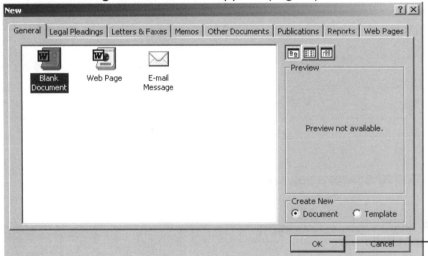

Blank Document is
automatically
highlighted in the **New**
dialogue box.

Click **OK** to create
a new blank
document.

Fig 10

T A S K

1.   *Ensure you are working in a new blank document.*

Inserting Text Into A New Document

To enter text into a new document, the cursor (insertion point) must be flashing in the work area. The flashing cursor determines the exact location where text will be inserted or editing actions will be carried out.

To move the cursor to another location within the document, move the mouse pointer to where you wish to start typing and double-click the left mouse button. Your flashing cursor will now appear in the new location ready for typing.

Entering text is normally carried out using the keyboard.

Word 2000 uses a word wrap facility, so there is no need to press the **Enter** key when you reach the end of the line. Word will do this for you and automatically wrap the text onto the next line. Press the **Enter** key twice (leaving one clear line) to start a new paragraph.

If mistakes are made when entering text, use the **Backspace** and the **Delete** key on the keyboard to correct.

The Backspace key deletes text appearing to the left of the cursor

The Delete key deletes text appearing to the right of the cursor

After a full stop or other punctuation at the end of a sentence, leave **two** clear spaces before typing the next sentence. One space is acceptable. However, you must be consistent, ie either always leave two spaces after the full stop or always leave one space.

T
A
S
K

1.   *Type the text below into the new document:*

> **Harvard Stationery Limited**
> **4 Stirling Road**
> **Winchester**
> **Lancashire**
> **W51 7YH**
>
> **[insert today's date]**
>
> **Dear Sirs,**
>
> **Re: Stationery Order Number 305**
>
> **Please find enclosed a cheque for £658.00. This is in full and final settlement of our order as above.**
>
> **Yours faithfully**
>
> **[leave 5 clear lines and type your name]**

Do not close - continued in the next task…

Selecting Text

When working with text in a document, many tasks will require the text to be selected (or highlighted) first. This is so that the application knows which piece of text to perform an action upon.

For example, to enhance a piece of text, for instance by making bold or underlined, select the text first and then click on the bold or underline button on the toolbar.

The selected or highlighted text in this example appears in the dark shading:

> Your name here
>
> Over the past year The Wildlife Club has been visiting Zoos and National Parks. Some are involved in the conservation of animals.

When the mouse pointer is moved over text in a document it will change in shape, instead of a pointer it will change to an I-Beam which looks like this: I

To select text

Point at the start of the text, press and hold the left mouse button, and drag the I-Beam over the text. This will highlight the text. Once the required text has been selected, release the mouse button.

or

Click at the start of the required text, press and hold the **Shift** key, use the arrow keys to select the required text. Once the required text has been selected, release the keys.

or

To select:

One word	Double-click with the mouse pointer (I-beam) anywhere on the word
One sentence	Press and hold the **Ctrl** button on the keyboard and click anywhere in the sentence.
One paragraph	Triple-click (3 clicks on the left mouse button) anywhere in the paragraph.

To **cancel** a selection, click anywhere in the work area of the Word window.

Working With Paragraphs

Inserting A New Paragraph

When entering text into a document, it can be divided into 'paragraphs'. A paragraph is created by typing a section of text and then separating it by pressing the **Enter** key twice.

When pressing the **Enter** key to create a new paragraph, Word inserts a paragraph mark (¶). However, this may be hidden from view. To display all paragraph marks in a document, click on the **Show/hide** button on the standard toolbar.

To hide the marks, click on the **Show/hide** button again.

When using the **Show/hide** button, spaces between words are shown as small dots and any manual page breaks can be viewed. A page break is where you have instructed the computer to start a new page within a document. The marks will not show on any printouts.

To join two paragraphs together, move the cursor to the end of the first paragraph (after the full stop) and press the **delete** button on the keyboard until the next paragraph joins it. Ensure that a space is left between the sentences at the join.

Another method is to move the cursor to the beginning of the second paragraph and press the **backspace** button until it joins the first paragraph.

Paragraphs have at least one clear line between them. To insert a new paragraph, move the cursor between existing paragraphs and press **Enter** twice to insert a clear line. Type the paragraph and ensure there is a clear line beneath it.

Saving Documents

Saving A Document To A Floppy Disk

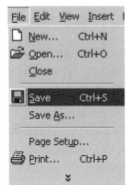

When saving a document, you are keeping it permanently and will be able to retrieve it at any time. The application allows you to name a document so as to identify and organise your documents clearly.

To save a new document, select **File**, **Save** from the menu bar (Fig 11) and the **Save As** dialogue box will be displayed (Fig 12). Alternatively, press **Ctrl+S** or **F12**.

Fig 11

All tasks carried out using this resource pack will be saved to 3½ Floppy (A:). Always ensure you have a floppy disk in the drive before attempting to save.

Once a document has been saved to disk, the file name will appear alongside the application name on the title bar. This is confirmation that the document has been saved correctly.

1. Click on the drop-down arrow to select the location to **Save in**.

Fig 12

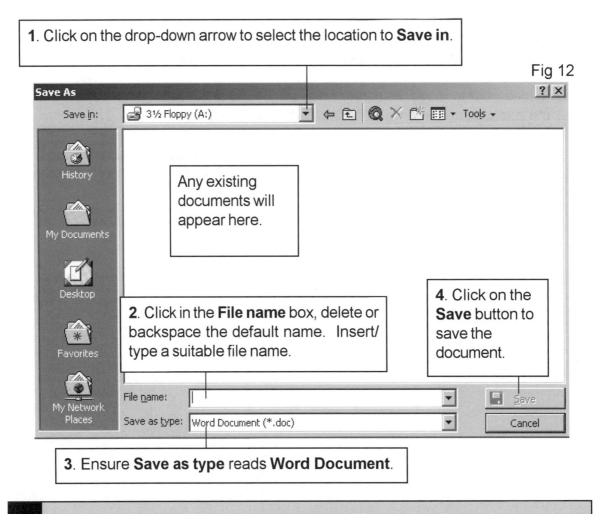

Any existing documents will appear here.

2. Click in the **File name** box, delete or backspace the default name. Insert/type a suitable file name.

4. Click on the **Save** button to save the document.

3. Ensure **Save as type** reads **Word Document**.

T A S K

1. Save the document as **Harvard Letter** to your floppy disk.

To save the document as you work, click **File**, **Save** from the menu bar. As the document has already been named and saved, no dialogue box will appear and any updates to the document will be saved. The document's name will remain the same.

Using the Save As command

It may be necessary to make amendments to a document and keep both the original and the updated version. The **Save As** command is used for this. By opening an existing document, amending or editing it and using **File**, **Save As** or **F12** from the menu bar, the document can be given a different name and both versions can be saved.

Once the **Save As** command has been used, the new document name will appear on the title bar.

Saving A Document To The Hard Disk

A similar procedure is used to save documents to the hard disk of the computer. The reasons to save to floppy disk or hard disk should be taken into consideration.

Saving to a floppy disk is useful as the disk is portable, it can be removed easily from the drive of the computer and taken to another computer in another location. However, floppy disks have a limited amount of space and therefore can fill up quite quickly.

An alternative is to save your documents to the computer's hard disk. This means that any documents stored will be located in the computer. This can be beneficial as the hard disk will have much more space than a floppy disk. However, the disk is not portable.

Computer disk drives are assigned a letter by the computer. The floppy disk drive is known as the A: drive and the hard disk is usually known as the C: drive. However, this can vary, depending on the computer system you are using.

> You are not required to complete this - **for information only**.

To save to the hard disk, click **File**, **Save** or **File**, **Save As** and select the location using the drop-down arrow as before (Fig 13).

If you are saving to folders, locate the required folder until it appears in the **Save in** box before clicking **Save**.

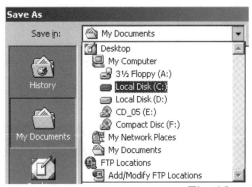

Fig 13

Saving A Document To A New Folder

When saving documents to either a floppy disk or a hard disk, it pays to be organised! For this purpose, documents can be saved or stored in 'folders'. Folders can be created on both floppy disks and hard disks and can be named.

For example, if you are storing letters, invoices, reports and newsletters on a floppy disk, it would be an advantage to have a folder for each type of document.

Folders can be created in Windows Explorer, a file management application. However, they can also be created in Microsoft Word when saving a document.

Click **File**, **Save As** (or **F12**).

The **Save As** dialogue box will appear (Fig 14). Click on the **New Folder** icon and the **New Folder** dialogue box will appear:

Fig 14

Type in a new name for your folder and click **OK**.

The new folder will appear in the **Save in** box.

T A S K	1.	*Save a copy of **Harvard Letter** to a new folder called **Letters**.*

Closing Documents

Closing A Word Document

Fig 15

Once you have finished working with a document, it is important to close it and exit the application. This will eliminate any risk of your work being lost or tampered with.

To close a document, use the menu bar (Fig 15).

Click **File** and **Close** (or **Ctrl+W**)

This will close down the active document and not Microsoft Word 2000.

Closing Microsoft Word 2000

Fig 16

To close Microsoft Word 2000, either use the menu bar (Fig 16) or the **close** button.

Click **File** and **Exit**.

To use the **close** button, locate the set of buttons at the very top right corner of the Word window, to the right of the title bar.

✂ Alternatively, press **Alt+F4**.

T
A
S

1. *Close your document.*

2. *Close Microsoft Word 2000.*

When using either of the above methods, you may receive a message asking if you would like to save any changes to a document (it may display the document name). If you have made any changes since the last save, click **Yes** (Fig 17).

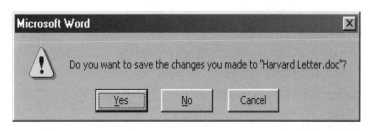

Fig 17

Opening Existing Documents

Opening Existing Documents

The document you are required to edit or amend may be an existing document. This means that the document has already been created and has been saved to a location either on the hard disk of the computer or on a floppy disk.

To open an existing document, click **File**, **Open** from the menu bar (Fig 18) to display the **Open** dialogue box (Fig 19).

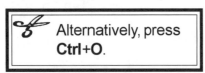 Alternatively, press **Ctrl+O**.

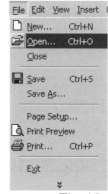

Fig 18

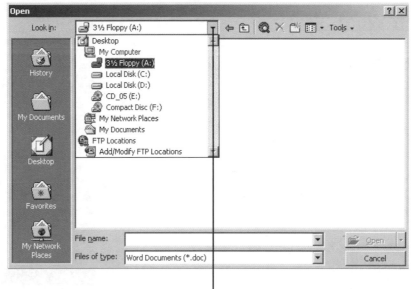

Fig 19

1. Select the location from the **Look in:** drop-down list (eg **3½ Floppy (A:)**).

2. Select the document required (eg Harvard Letter).

3. Click on the **Open** button.

Once open, the document will appear as it was last saved.

To modify or edit the document by adding text, place the cursor in the location where the text is to be added.

When editing or updating an existing document, it may be necessary to insert extra space to accommodate the additional text which may be required.

TASK

1. *Open the existing document **Harvard Letter** from within the **Letters** folder.*

Switching Between Open Word Documents

Microsoft Word 2000 is capable of opening more than one document at any one time. You may be required to work in this way when needing to refer to more than one document, or taking data from one to put into another.

To open an existing document, use the procedure covered on the previous page.

Select the required document and click **Open**. An indication of which document is active (open) will appear on the title bar.

Blank new documents can also be opened.

The most recently opened document will appear active in the Word window, hiding any previously opened documents.

To switch between the active or open documents, use the **Window** menu on the menu bar (Fig 20).

The **Window** menu will display which documents are active or open at any one time.

A tick will appear next to the document which is currently active (displayed in the Word window).

Fig 20

To view another document, click on the document name in the list.

To view other programmes press **Alt+Tab**. A small dialogue box will appear displaying all active programmes.

You can switch between programmes by successively pressing the **Tab** key until the box appears around the programme you wish to view.

T A S K	1.	*Open a blank new document.*
	2.	*Practise switching between the open documents.*
	3.	*Close the blank new document. Do not save any changes.*

Creating A Back Up Copy

When saving to a floppy disk or hard disk, it is essential to 'back up' your work. This means to create copies of your documents and store them for safe keeping. Floppy disks can damage easily, as they are susceptible to dust if not stored in the correct manner (stored in a floppy disk holder and covered).

Backing up files which are stored on your computer's hard disk is also very important. The computer is at risk from viruses which can corrupt the system files which work your computer. It is also at risk of hard disk failure or corruption or even theft or power failure.

A regular routine of backing up your documents is all that is required for peace of mind. Set a date each week or month to back up and store the copied files in a safe place, clearly and fully marking what is contained on the disk.

For basic back up procedures, floppy disks can be used. However, if you have many documents which take up a lot of space, another method should be considered, such as a CD writer or a tape back up system.

To save a back up copy of a document to a floppy disk:

- **Open** the document to be backed up.

- Click **File**, **Save** (or Ctrl+S) to ensure all amendments have been saved and are up-to-date.

- Click **File**, **Save As** (or F12) to display the **Save As** dialogue box.

- Select the **3½ Floppy (A:)** from the **Save in:** drop-down list.

- Type in an appropriate **File name** to identify the document as the back up, for example: **myfilebackup.doc** (the file extension '.doc' will automatically be added by the computer).

- Ensure the **Save as type:** box displays **Word Document**.

- Click on the **Save** button.

- Notice the title bar will display the new file name (ie the back up copy). Close the document once backed up.

> **myfilebackup.doc - Microsoft Word**

T A S K	1.	*Create a back up copy of the **Harvard Letter** with a suitable name and save to your floppy disk.*
	2.	*Save the back up copy to the folder called **Letters**.*
	3.	*Close the document.*

T
A
S
K

1.   *Start a new blank document and type in the following text:*

Meeting Discussion Points

Office Layouts

Desks

All members of staff who are moving to the new offices are to have their desks dismantled, boxed and ready for the move date. Any broken desks are to be reported to a Supervisor who will arrange for them to be replaced.

Computers

All staff expressing an interest in receiving the new software are to advise a Supervisor as soon as possible. A new computer system will be reserved, provided a business case for having the new software is produced. Any existing computer faults must be reported to a Supervisor or the I.T. Department as soon as possible.

Facilities

Staff facilities are available in the new building for all departments. Staff are asked to adhere to using their own facilities. All departments are to be responsible for their own refreshments and personal items.

Departments

Office Space

Appropriate office space has been provided for all departments. Should a department wish to expand its area due to lack of space, this must be cleared with a Supervisor. No item of equipment is to be moved without express permission.

Equipment

All equipment has been marked and recorded. A check has been put into place and will take place after the move. Any damage to equipment must be reported.

Conference Facilities

There are two conference rooms available in the new building. Any department wishing to book the rooms must do so through the main building reception, where a book will be kept. The rooms must be kept clean and tidy at all times, as clients will be using the rooms.

2.   *Save the document to your floppy disk as **Meeting**.*

3.   *Close the document.*

On completion of this unit, you will have learnt about and practised the following:

- **Page Layout**

  - Page Setup
  - Margins
  - Gutters

- **Printing**

  - Printing A Document
  - Print Preview A Document

- **Adding Document Information**

  - Adding Page Numbers
  - Headers And Footers
  - Alignment Of Headers And Footers
  - Editing Headers And Footers
  - Removing Page Numbers From Headers And Footers

Page Layout

Page Setup

When producing a document, it is important to consider its presentation, ie how the document is required to look in respect of orientation, paper size, margin widths etc. To set this type of criteria for a document, **Page Setup** is used. The **Page Setup** dialogue box will allow a document to be adjusted according to requirements such as paper size, orientation and margins.

Select **File**, **Page Setup** from the menu bar and the **Page Setup** dialogue box (Fig 21) will be displayed.

Ensure the **Paper Size** tab is selected:

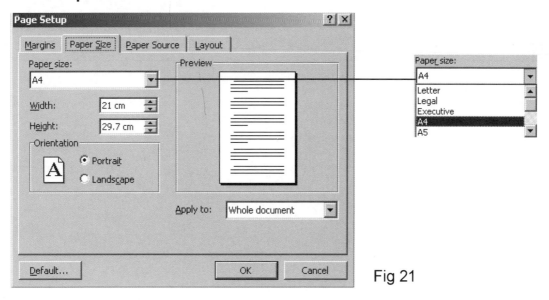

Fig 21

To change the paper size, click on the drop-down arrow and select the size required.

The dialogue box contains a **Preview** pane. When applying any settings, check that the preview looks correct before clicking **OK**.

To abandon the settings, click on the **Cancel** button.

Page Orientation

Orientation is the way in which the document will print on paper. There are two ways:

Portrait   Documents in portrait format will have the short edge of the paper appearing at the top.

Landscape   Documents in landscape format will have the long edge of the paper appearing at the top.

T A S K

1. Open the document called **Meeting**.

2. View the page setup for the document.

   Answer the following questions on a separate sheet of paper:

3. View the paper size options for the document. How many and what options are there?

4. What is the difference in measurement between A4 size and letter size?

5. When you select a different paper size, which section of the dialogue box will show the updated changes?

6. What orientation would you recommend for this document and why?

<u>Margins</u>

The purpose of margins when working in a word processed document is to control the amount of space between the text and the edge of the paper. Imagine a document with no margin area. When printed, the document text would appear too close or even over the edge of the paper. It is for this reason that a margin area is set, giving a neat edge or frame around the page.

There are four margins, **Top**, **Bottom**, **Left** and **Right**. In Fig 22 below, notice the horizontal and vertical ruler bars.

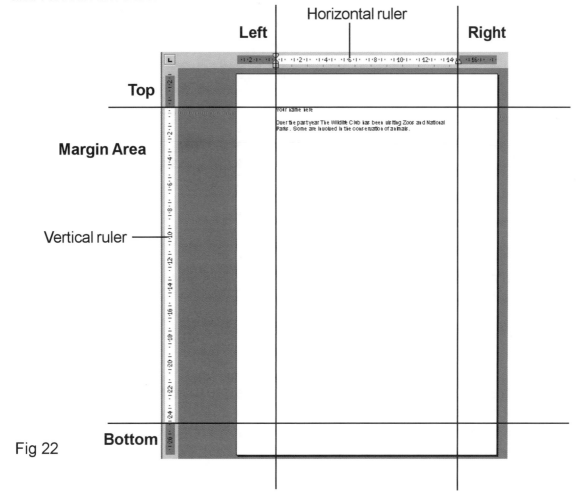

Fig 22

The ruler bars will display the measurement unit used, either inches or centimetres.

To change the measurement units, select **Tools**, **Options** from the menu bar.

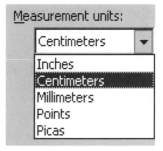

Locate the **General** tab. At the bottom of the dialogue box is an option to change the measurement units.

Click on the drop-down arrow to change and click **OK** to apply or **Cancel** to abandon.

To adjust the margins, select **File**, **Page Setup** (Fig 23) from the menu bar and select the **Margins** tab. Alternatively double click on the **Ruler** bar.

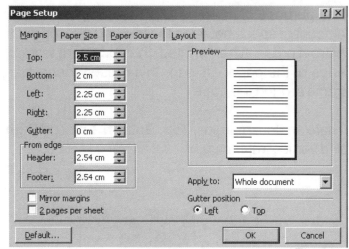

Notice the existing margin settings, together with a **Preview** pane. Each time a margin setting is changed, the preview will be updated.

Fig 23

New measurements can be set by clicking on the upper or lower arrows appearing next to the measurement. As they are clicked, the measurement will change. However, using this method will increase or decrease the measurement in 10ths of a centimetre (cm).

If a specific measurement is required, click three times with the left mouse button on the existing value, this will highlight it.

Type in the new measurement.

When inputting margin measurements, never insert the CM for centimetres or any symbols for inches. By setting the measurement unit required using Tools and Options, the application will automatically add them for you.

To apply the new measurements, click **OK**. To abandon, click **Cancel**.

Gutters

Gutters are the amount of space that is left for binding a document such as a booklet like the one you are reading now.

Extra space is added to the left margin of all pages if the **Mirror margins** check box has been cleared.

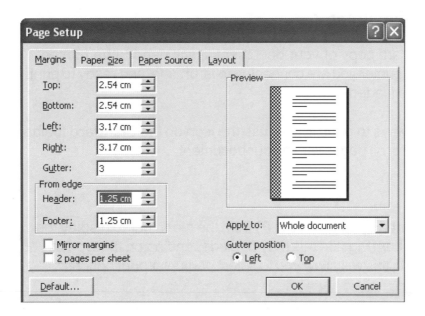

Notice the **Gutter** box above in the **Margins** dialogue box. A value of 3cm has been added to the gutter measurement. The Gutter position has been set at Left, and this means that the preview will display the patterned Gutter position to the left (left margin) of the page.

Gutters can also be top aligned, depending on how your book will be opened and read.

T A S K

1. Open the document called **Meeting**.

2. Set the page to portrait orientation.

3. Change the margins to the following:

    Top 3cm
    Bottom 3cm
    Left 2.5cm
    Right 2.5cm

4. Save the changes.

Printing

Printing A Document

To produce a hard copy of your document, it will need to be printed. It is important to ensure that the printer you are connected to is 'on-line' and ready to print. Also ensure the correct paper is loaded.

There are two ways to print. Either use the icon on the **Standard** toolbar, 🖨 which will produce a print of all pages within your document,

or

select **File**, **Print** (Fig 24) (or **Ctrl+P**) from the menu bar to display the **Print** dialogue box (Fig 25 - this may differ depending on the type of printer installed); this will allow you to select particular print options.

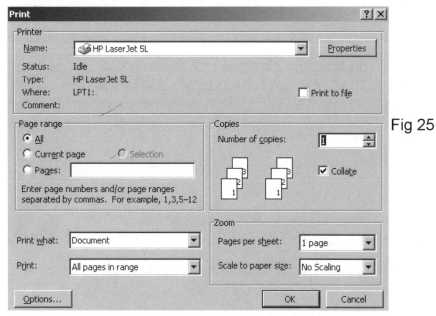

Fig 24

Fig 25

Set the required criteria for your print then click **OK** to proceed.

Click **Cancel** to abandon the print.

Notice that the dialogue box is split into various sections:

Printer	This will display the current printer you are connected to. If you are connected to more than one printer, it will be displayed in the drop-down list. However, this should not need to be changed.
Page range	You can select which pages of the document are to be printed; the current page, a selection or certain pages.
Copies	Select the number of copies required and whether they are required to be collated (gathered) into sets.
Zoom	Zoom will allow you to print more than one page from your document to a sheet of paper and scale to a certain paper size.
Print what & Print	These sections allow you to print certain criteria of the document, such as only odd pages or only even pages.

Print Preview A Document

Microsoft Word 2000 has a facility called **Print Preview**. This is accessible by clicking on the **Print Preview** button on the standard toolbar or by selecting **File**, **Print Preview** from the menu bar (or **Ctrl+F2**).

The purpose of print preview is to display the document as it will look when printed. By using this feature before you print, the document can be checked for layout, orientation and margins etc. Viewing a page before printing saves a wasted print, ie paper and ink. Print preview is known as a **WYSIWYG** feature (**W**hat **Y**ou **S**ee **I**s **W**hat **Y**ou **G**et); the document that you see on screen will match the printed document.

Print preview will open in its own window and has its own toolbar (Fig 26). To return back to your document, click on the **Close** button.

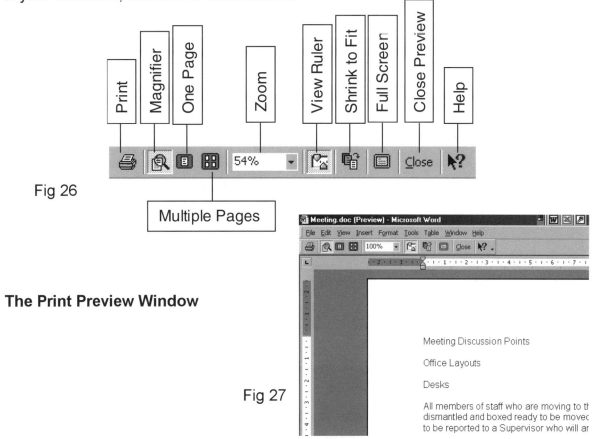

Fig 26

Multiple Pages

The Print Preview Window

Fig 27

Notice in Fig 27 that the document name will still appear on the title bar. However, the word 'Preview' will also appear in brackets to indicate that you are previewing the document. The document will appear as it will be printed on paper. You cannot edit the document in print preview.

T A S K	1.	*Preview the document called **Meeting**.*
	2.	*Print the document.*
	3.	*Open the document called **Harvard Letter**, print and close.*

Adding Document Information

Document information includes adding items such as page numbering, page totalling, headers and footers. Page numbering will add each page number to a certain position on a page and will display when printed. Page totalling will give information on how many pages there are in total in your document on every page, such as Page 1 of 1 (1/1) or Page 2 of 6 (2/6) etc.

When adding a header or footer, information regarding the document will appear at the top (header) or at the bottom (footer). Both can display useful information such as the file name, date and time, or custom information on every page.

Adding Page Numbers

To add page numbering to a document, click on **Insert**, **Page Numbers** from the menu bar. This will display the **Page Numbers** dialogue box (Fig 28).

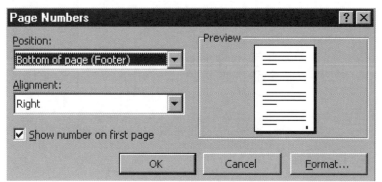

Fig 28

Select the position for the page numbers, ie at the top of the page (header) or the bottom of the page (footer).

Select the alignment and whether to include the page number on the first page.

If a particular numbering format is required such as Roman numerals, click on the **Format** button to display the **Page Number Format** dialogue box (Fig 29).

To edit or delete page numbering, the header or footer is used to access it. See the next section on Headers and Footers.

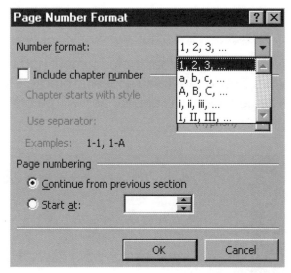

Fig 29

Headers And Footers

Headers will appear at the top of each page in a document; footers will appear at the bottom of each page in a document. They can include text or graphics - for example, page numbers, the date, a company logo, the document's title or file name, or the author's name. A header is printed in the top margin; a footer is printed in the bottom margin.

You can use the same header and footer throughout a document or change the header and footer for part of the document. For example, use a unique header or footer on the first page, or leave the header or footer off the first page. You can also use different headers and footers on odd and even pages or for part of a document.

Fig 30 displays an example of headers and footers.

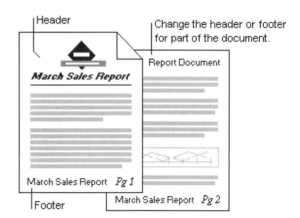

Fig 30

To insert a header and/or footer, click **View**, **Header and Footer** from the menu bar.

The document will appear in **Print Layout** View as in Fig 31 below.

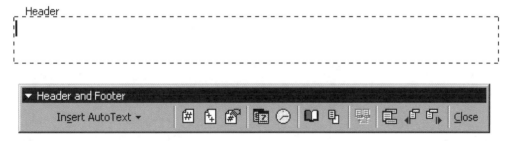

Fig 31

The **Header and Footer** toolbar will appear and any text within your document will appear grey.

The **Header and Footer** toolbar contains buttons which will insert criteria for you, for example the page number, the time and the date.

Insert AutoText will allow you to insert any pre-defined information such as a company name, author name or logo etc, which has previously been added using AutoText.

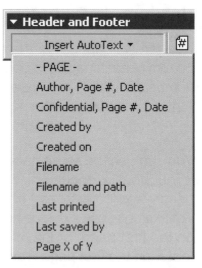

To insert AutoText, click on the button to display a drop-down list of available text entries.

If you have customised AutoText entries such as a company name, it will appear here.

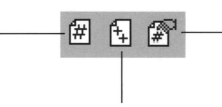

Insert Page Number ——— **Format Page Number** (displays the **Page Number Format** dialogue box - Fig 29)

Insert Number of Pages

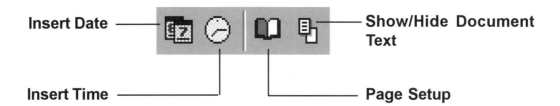

Insert Date ——— **Show/Hide Document Text**

Insert Time ——— **Page Setup**

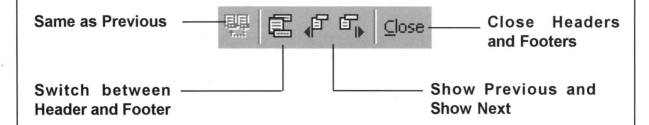

Same as Previous ——— **Close Headers and Footers**

Switch between Header and Footer ——— **Show Previous and Show Next**

When all required criteria have been added to the header and/or footer, click on the close button on the **Header and Footer** toolbar to return to your document.

T A S K	1.	*Edit the document called **Meeting**.*
	2.	*Add a header to include the page number.*
	3.	*Add a footer to include the filename (AutoText) and the date.*
	4.	*Save the changes.*

Page Totals

Page totals are used to add information into the header and footer about the number of total pages in a document. For example, you may have a 50-page document and be viewing page 10, the status bar at the bottom of the Word screen will indicate that you are viewing Page 10/50 (page 10 of a total of 50 pages). However, if total page numbers have not been added in the header or the footer of the document when it is printed, there will be no indication of which page is which.

To insert the total number of pages in a header or footer, activate the Header and Footer by clicking on **View**, **Header And Footer** from the Menu bar:

View either the header or footer, ready to insert your total page numbers.

Type in the word 'Page' and notice that a small Screen Tip will appear, stating Page X of Y, this indicates that by pressing **Enter** you can accept to total the page numbers, Page 1 of 13 for example.

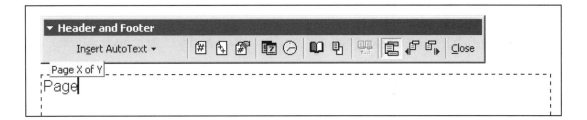

Once this has been accepted, the header or footer will appear as shown below:

Click on **close** to close the header and footer and the page totals will appear greyed out at the end or beginning of each new page.

<u>Alignment Of Headers And Footers</u>

When a header or footer has been activated, markers will appear on the ruler bar. The markers are tab stop positions and by default, one will appear at the centre of the header and footer and one will appear at the extreme right.

Using the tab stop positions will enable you to enter more than one item into a document's header and footer. Look at the examples below. Fig 32 shows the tab stop positions on the ruler bar, and Fig 33 is an example of different criteria entered against the positions.

When entering more than one criteria into either the header or footer, use the following steps:

1.   Enter the first criteria.

2.   Press the **Tab** key on the keyboard (to reach the first tab stop position).

3.   Enter the second criteria.

4.   Press the **Tab** key on the keyboard (to reach the second tab stop position).

5.   Enter the third criteria.

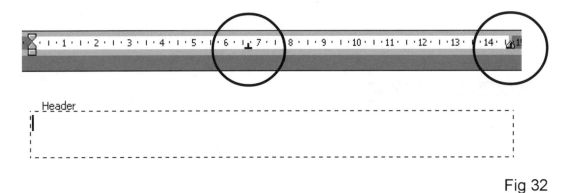

Fig 32

Fig 33

Editing Headers And Footers

To edit, amend or add to criteria contained within a header or footer, select **View**, **Header and Footer** from the menu bar as previously.

Depending upon your requirements, add criteria or amend existing criteria. To select different formats for numbers or to delete them, for example, highlight the numbers and select **Format Page Number** from the **Header and Footer** toolbar. This will activate the **Page Number Format** dialogue box (Fig 29 - page 42).

When all required criteria have been added to the header and/or footer, click on the **close** button on the **Header and Footer** toolbar to return to your document.

T A S K

1. *Format the page number in the header to lower case Roman numerals eg i, ii, iii, iv.*

2. *Insert the following text below the existing text:*

> **Recreation Area**
>
> **Notice Boards**
>
> **Notice boards have been provided in one central area for all departments. Subject areas for notices will include staff events, staff training, charity organisations, sporting events and meetings. Any member of staff wishing to add an item of information to the notice board will require permission from a Supervisor before displaying it.**
>
> **Responsibilities**
>
> **The new building is the responsibility of all staff. Any untoward occurrences are to be reported to a Supervisor, ie issues regarding security of staff or equipment.**
>
> **Health and Safety**
>
> **All members of staff are responsible for their own health and safety at work. Safety workshops will be provided later in the year; any volunteers to take the workshops will be appreciated. All staff must be vigilant in making themselves aware of the Health and Safety at Work Act. Information will be provided on the notice board in the recreation area regarding this issue. All staff are to read the notice board regularly.**

3. *Print the document.*

4. *Save changes to the document and close.*

Removing Page Numbers From Headers And Footer

To remove any information from a header or footer, activate the header and footer by clicking on **View**, **Header and Footer** from the menu bar.

Click into the header or footer and edit the text as required. This can be edited as with normal text; notice that the formatting toolbar is activated. You can highlight (select) text and numbers in either the header or footer and delete as required.

If page numbers are deleted, they will be deleted from every page in the document.

If you wish to delete the page number from the first page of a document but leave them on all remaining pages, use the **Page Numbers** dialogue box, and uncheck the box titled **Show number on first page**.

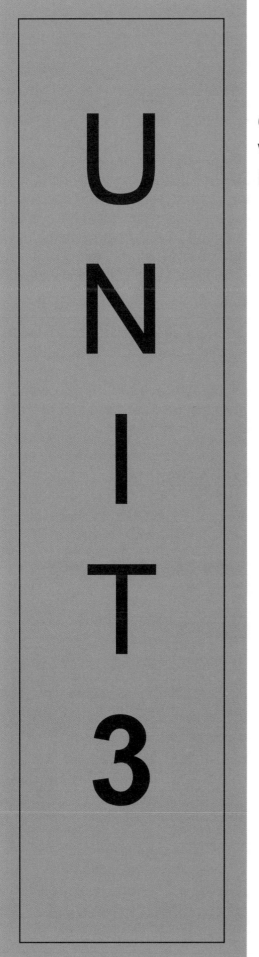

On completion of this unit, you will have learnt about and practised the following:

- **Working With Templates**

  - What Are Templates?
  - Creating A New Template From An Existing Template
  - Saving Templates
  - Creating A New Document From A Template Stored On A Floppy Disk

Working With Templates

What Are Templates?

Every Microsoft Word document is based on a template. A template determines the basic structure for a document and contains document settings such as fonts, page layout, special formatting and styles.

The two basic types of templates are global templates and document templates. Global templates, including the normal template, contain settings that are available to all documents. Document templates, such as the memo or fax templates, contain settings that are available only to documents based on those templates. For example, if you create a memo using the memo template, the memo will use the preset fonts and styles etc, letting you add your required text. Word provides a variety of document templates and you can create your own document templates.

There is a variety of templates available in Word 2000 for documents such as letters, memoranda, faxes and reports.

A template can be customised to include your own personal criteria such as the company name, address and logo. This is then saved as a template and can be used over and over again as a basis for all documents thereafter.

Creating A New Template From An Existing Template

To create a new template click **File**, **New** from the menu bar to activate the **New** dialogue box (Fig 34).

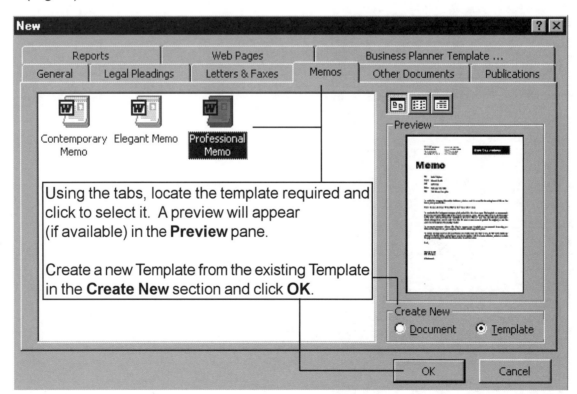

Fig 34

The existing template will appear, ready to be edited with custom information (fig 35).

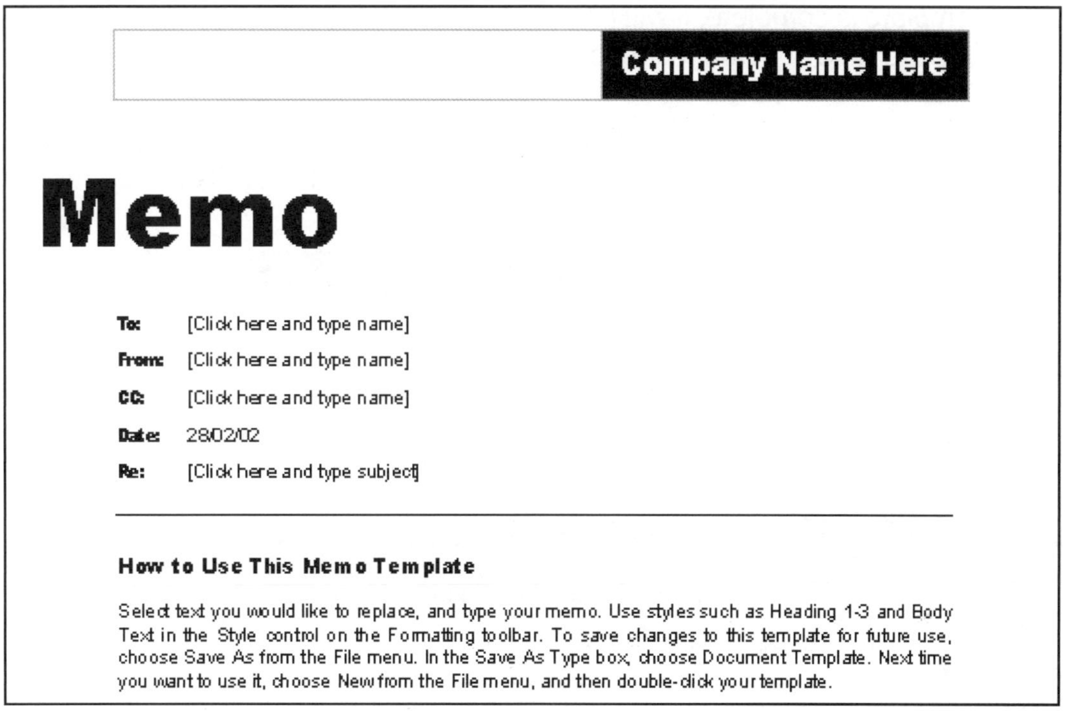

Company Name Here

Memo

To: [Click here and type name]

From: [Click here and type name]

CC: [Click here and type name]

Date: 28/02/02

Re: [Click here and type subject]

How to Use This Memo Template

Select text you would like to replace, and type your memo. Use styles such as Heading 1-3 and Body Text in the Style control on the Formatting toolbar. To save changes to this template for future use, choose Save As from the File menu. In the Save As Type box, choose Document Template. Next time you want to use it, choose New from the File menu, and then double-click your template.

Fig 35

The template will display instructions on how to edit it to display your own custom information.

TASK

1. *Create a new template based on the **Professional Memo** template.*
2. *Add the company name: **Outsource Limited**.*

Saving Templates

When the template is complete, it will need to be saved to a location to be retrieved whenever you create a document based on it.

The title bar at the top of the Word 2000 screen gives information regarding the active document you are working in. If you are working in a template, it will display information similar to Fig 36 below.

Template1 - Memo - Microsoft Word   Fig 36

To save the template, click **File**, **Save As** (or **F12**) from the menu bar to display the **Save As** dialogue box (Fig 37). Notice that the **Filename** and **Save as Type** boxes display differently compared with that of saving a normal document.

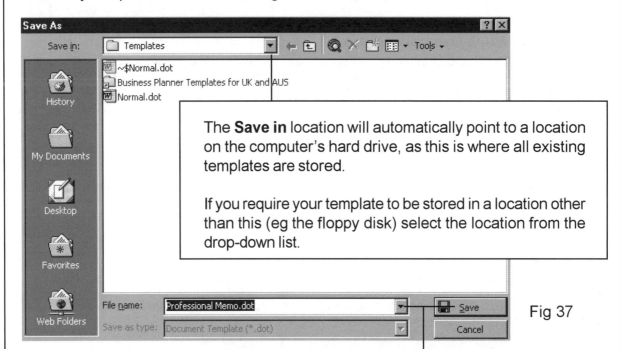

The **Save in** location will automatically point to a location on the computer's hard drive, as this is where all existing templates are stored.

If you require your template to be stored in a location other than this (eg the floppy disk) select the location from the drop-down list.

Fig 37

The **file name** will automatically appear, together with a special file extension for template files. To edit this, click into the **File name** box and type the required name for the template.

Use logical names such as 'Letter Template' or 'Memo Template'.

To save the template, click on the **Save** button.

In the above example, the memo has now been saved as a template. In order to create future memos using the template, it must always be opened from the original template and created as a new document.

T
A
S
K

1. *Save as a template with the name **Memo_Temp** to your floppy disk.*

2. *Close the template.*

NB Saving template files into the **Templates** folder will result in the templates being displayed in the **General** section of the **New** dialogue box. For the purposes of this resource pack we will request that all templates are saved to a floppy disk.

Creating A New Document From A Template Stored On A Floppy Disk

To recap, an existing Word 2000 template has been edited to include custom information. This has been saved as a custom template for use with a new document.

To create a new document from the template:

1. Click **File**, **New** (or **Ctrl+N**) from the menu bar to display the **New** dialogue box (Fig 38).

2. Select the **General** tab.

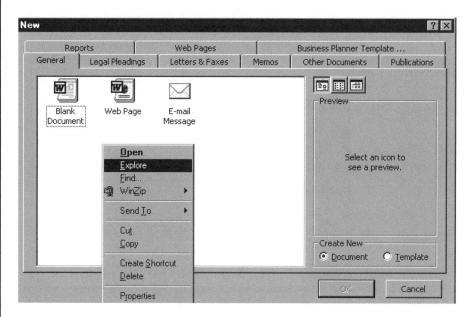

Fig 38

3. Move the cursor to a white part of the **New** dialogue box and click on the right mouse button. Select **Explore** from the sub-menu.

4. Windows Explorer will open. Select **3½ Floppy (A:)** and double-click on the template required.

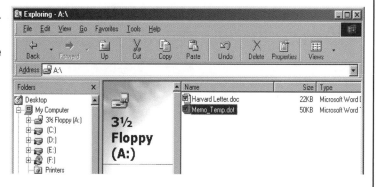

5. Before the document will open, click **Cancel** on the **New** dialogue box.

T A S K

1. Use the **Memo_Temp** template to create the memo document below.

To: All Staff

From: John O'Shea - Supervisor

CC: Directors

Date: 07/03/02

Re: Charity Event – Sports Day

Silly Sports Day

I am happy to announce that the 'Silly Sports Day' is here again! Any staff wishing to enter a team are to write their names on this memo within 7 days. We are looking for 5 teams in total.

Events are as follows:

'Silly sack' race

'Carry as much as you can' race

'Billy Bobs Stick' race

'The Pie in your Face' race

In addition to the above, there will be a competition for the best dressed team - the more outrageous the costume the better!

---

2. Print the document.

3. Save the memo as **Memo Sports** to a new folder called **Memoranda** on your floppy disk.

4. Close the document.

CONSOLIDATION EXERCISE

Your Supervisor has asked you to produce a template to be used as a base for letters sent to all staff within the company - Outsource Limited.

1. *Produce a template using the **Professional Letter** template. The template should include the following information:*

Company Name:	**Outsource Limited**
Company Address:	**10-11 Vernon Way**
	Winchester
	Lancashire
	WH7 9LK
Tel No:	**01485 1166542**
Name:	**John O'Shea**
Job Title:	**Supervisor**

2. *Format the page setup of the template to portrait with margins, top & bottom: 3cm, left & right: 3.2cm.*

3. *Produce a printed output of the template and save it using the name **Outsource_temp** to a new folder called **Outsource Letters** on your floppy disk.*

4. *Close the template.*

5. *Use the template created above to create the following letter. Names and addresses of all staff will be inserted later.*

> **Dear Sir or Madam:**
>
> **Please find attached a map showing the location of the new office block. Any staff who are moving to the new block are to report to a meeting on 25 January 2002 to discuss this.**
>
> **If any member of staff is unable to attend the meeting, please inform me as soon as possible.**

6. *Leave 3 clear lines below the signature line and insert the letters 'Enc' to show that the letter will have an enclosure.*

7. *Add a footer to the document to include the **Filename** and **Path Autotext**.*

8. *Save the letter as **L1OfficeMove** to the folder **Outsource Letters**.*

9. *Print the letter and close, saving any additional changes.*

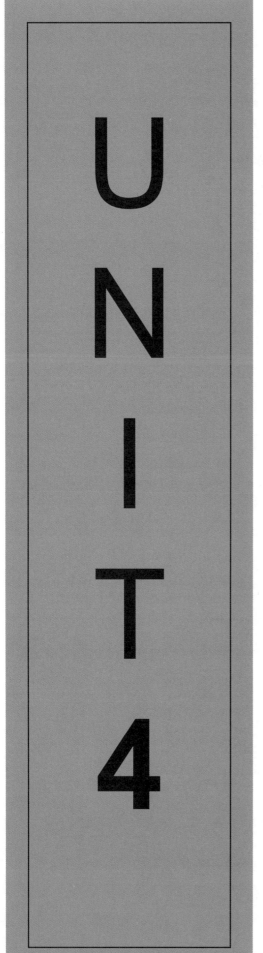

On completion of this unit, you will have learnt about and practised the following:

- **Text Enhancement**

  - Formatting Fonts
  - Applying Attributes To Text
  - The Font Dialogue Box
  - Format Painter
  - Text Alignment
  - Character Spacing
  - Borders And Shading Text
  - Working With Styles
  - Types Of Style
  - Applying Existing Styles To Text
  - Creating A New Style

- **Text Placement**

  - Cutting, Copying And Pasting Within A Document
  - Cutting, Copying And Pasting Between Documents
  - Deleting Text

Text Enhancement

Formatting Fonts

A font is a typeface; the appearance of the characters. Microsoft Word 2000 offers many different font types and each font has a name such as Arial, Times New Roman and Tahoma.

In addition to changing the type of font, the font size can also be changed. Font size is measured in points. One point is equal to 1/72 of an inch. An average document uses a font size of between 8 and 14 points. However, headings may be formatted to a larger size.

One method of formatting the font and font size is to use the formatting toolbar:

To change the font, select the text and click on the drop-down arrow to the right of the **Font** box on the **Formatting** toolbar (Fig 39) (or **Ctrl+Shift+F**).

Fig 39

To change the font size, select the text and click on the drop-down arrow to the right of the **Size** box on the **Formatting** toolbar (Fig 40) (or **Ctrl+Shift+P**).

Fig 40

Both of the above methods can be carried out to the same piece of text whilst it is selected.

Applying Attributes To Text

Attributes such as **Bold**, <u>Underline</u> and *Italic* can be applied using the formatting toolbar. After selecting text, click on a button to apply. Here are some examples (known as text enhancement).

B	Bold	(**Ctrl+B**)
U	<u>Underline</u>	(**Ctrl+U**)
I	*Italic*	(**Ctrl+I**)

The buttons act in a similar way to an 'on' and 'off' switch, ie to activate or switch the bold attribute on, highlight/select the text and click on the **Bold** button on the toolbar. To remove bold, highlight/select the text and click again on the **Bold** button.

The Font Dialogue Box

Another method of formatting the font and applying attributes to text is to select **Format**, **Font** from the menu bar. This will display the **Font** dialogue box (Fig 41) (or **Ctrl+D**).

Additional formatting can be carried out using this method, such as embossing and shadowing text.

Select or highlight text before applying any formatting from the **Font** dialogue box.

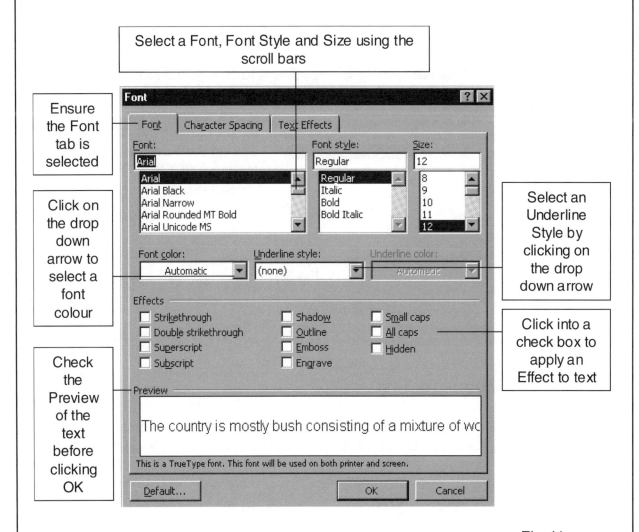

Fig 41

Format Painter

The **Format Painter** tool on the standard toolbar allows you to apply a set of formats at once to another piece of text.

All headings may be required to follow the format previously applied to some text (eg Arial, size 16pt, bold and blue in colour). To utilise the formatting previously applied to specific text, it is quicker to use format painter.

To use format painter:

1.   Click into the heading with formatting applied.

2.   Double-click the **Format Painter** toolbar button to activate.

3.   Click onto each remaining heading in turn.

      The mouse pointer will have changed to a symbol of a paintbrush to indicate that format painter is activated.

4.   To switch off the format painter option, click on the **Format Painter** tool on the toolbar.

T
A
S
K

1.   *Open the document called **Meeting** for editing.*

2.   *Format the main heading 'Meeting Discussion Points' to Arial, size 16pt, bold and shadow.*

3.   *Format the headings 'Office Layouts', 'Departments' and 'Recreation Area' to Arial size 14pt, bold.*

4.   *Format all remaining headings to Arial, size 12pt, bold, italic and the colour violet.*

5.   *Ensure all remaining paragraph text is Arial, size 12pt.*

6.   *Save the changes to the document.*

7.   *Print and close the document.*

Text Alignment

Text alignment will depend on the layout requirements of the document being produced. For example, if you are creating a menu for a restaurant on a single A4 piece of paper, you will typically align the text centred. This means that each line of text will be 'aligned' with the centre of the page.

Text alignment is the way the left and right ends of the text are aligned against the margin. This example demonstrates the four types of alignment applied to the same paragraph copied four times:

Left
align
(**Ctrl+L**)

Chester Zoo has an excellent web site, stating that it is dedicated to 'Saving animal species from extinction.' It also states that 'The role of the Zoo is to support and promote conservation by breeding threatened animals, by excellent animal welfare, high quality public service, recreation, education and science.'

Centre
(**Ctrl+E**)

Chester Zoo have an excellent web site, stating that it is dedicated to 'Saving animal species from extinction.' It also states that 'The role of the Zoo is to support and promote conservation by breeding threatened animals, by excellent animal welfare, high quality public service, recreation, education and science.'

Right
align
(**Ctrl+R**)

Chester Zoo have an excellent web site, stating that it is dedicated to 'Saving animal species from extinction.' It also states that 'The role of the Zoo is to support and promote conservation by breeding threatened animals, by excellent animal welfare, high quality public service, recreation, education and science.'

Justify
(**Ctrl+J**)

Chester Zoo have an excellent web site, stating that it is dedicated to 'Saving animal species from extinction.' It also states that 'The role of the Zoo is to support and promote conservation by breeding threatened animals, by excellent animal welfare, high quality public service, recreation, education and science.'

To apply alignment to text, select the text and click on an alignment button on the formatting toolbar.

Align Left

Centre

Align Right

Justify

T
A
S
K

1. Start a new blank document.

2. Create the memo below, using the memo template previously created.

To:	All Staff
From:	Roger Jones
CC:	Directors
Date:	08/03/02
Re:	Building Repairs

Please note that from the end of next week, repairs will be carried out to the roof area of building 3. Safety fencing and additional signage will be erected to alert all members of staff in the area.

The building company will be working with extremely hot substances and the safety of all staff is of the utmost importance. Please be alert whilst the work is carried out.

We apologise for any inconvenience caused during the works. However, we are sure that all staff understand the importance of the work.

3. Format the font of the memo text to Arial, size 14pt.

4. Format the third paragraph to bold and centred.

5. Format the first and second paragraphs to left aligned.

6. Save the memo as **Memo Building** to the **Memoranda** folder.

7. Print the document.

8. Close the document.

Character Spacing

Character spacing can be used when text in a document needs to fit specifically into a certain area, or to enhance its appearance on a page. It allows a piece of text, formatted with the same font and size as the remaining text, to be spaced differently widthways across the page.

Here are some examples of horizontally spaced characters:

> This is horizontal spacing at 66%
> This is horizontal spacing at 90%
> This is horizontal spacing at 100%

All of the above lines of text have been formatted to Arial, 20pt. However, the horizontal spacing of text has been set at various percentages so that characters appear either closer together or further apart.

To adjust character spacing for a selected piece of text, click on **Format**, **Font** from the Menu bar and select the **Character Spacing** tab:

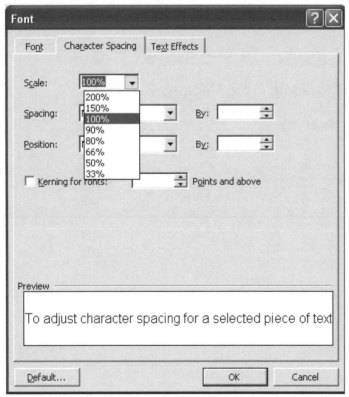

The **Scale** box drop-down list displays a number of scale percentages that are used to adjust the horizontal spacing of text.

You can also adjust the spacing and position of text by using the **Spacing** and **Position** boxes below the Scale box. Options include Expanded or Condensed.

The **Preview** box will display how the text will look with the settings you have chosen.

To apply them, click on **OK**.

Bordering And Shading Text

There are many ways in which text can be enhanced and made to stand out and appear more eye-catching with the use of different fonts and font sizes, spacing and attributes such as bold, underline and Italic. Other methods of enhancing text are the application of borders and shading.

Borders

To apply a border to a piece of text, highlight the text.

Select **Format**, **Borders and Shading** from the Menu bar:

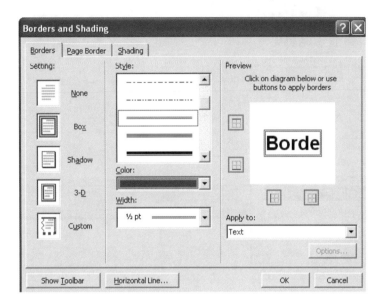

The dialogue box is split into three sections:

Setting:

Click to select the type of border line to use around the text selected. Options include a box, a shadowed box, 3D and custom.

Style:

Choose the line style, ie single line, dotted, double-line and the thickness and colour in this section.

Preview:

The preview will display the text and border you have selected.

Ensure the **Apply to** box displays 'text', as borders and shading can be applied to many other items inserted into a Word document.

Once you have selected all the options required, click on the **OK** button to apply them.

Shading:

Shading can be applied to appear behind the text, and this looks particularly attractive when a border has also been applied.

Select **Format**, **Borders and Shading** from the menu bar.

Click on the **Shading** tab.

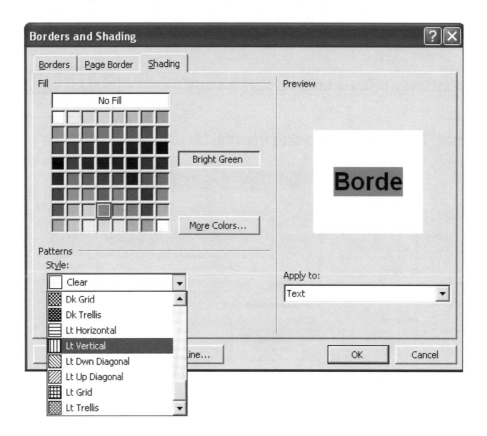

The dialogue box is split into three sections: **Fill**, **Patterns** and **Preview**.

Fill:
Select the colour of the fill background to the text that you require.

Patterns:
Browse through various colours and patterns to appear behind the text. Be careful not to obscure text using this feature.

Preview:
The preview will display the text and shading you have selected.

Ensure the **Apply to** box displays 'text', since borders and shading can be applied to many other items inserted into a Word document.

Once you have selected all the options required, click on the **OK** button to apply them.

Working With Styles

A style is a set of formatting characteristics that you can apply to text in your document to change its appearance. When you apply a style, you apply a whole group of formats in one simple task.

For example, you may want to format the title of a document to make it stand out. Instead of taking three separate steps to format your title as 16pt, Arial and centre-aligned, you can achieve the same result in one step by applying the **Title** style.

When starting Microsoft Word, the new blank document is based on the Normal template and text that you type uses the **Normal** style. This means that when you start typing, Word uses the font, font size, line spacing, text alignment and other formats currently defined for the **Normal** style. The **Normal** style is the base style for the **Normal** template, meaning that it is a foundation for other styles in the template.

There are a number of other styles besides **Normal** available in the Normal template. A few basic ones are shown in the **Style** list on the **Formatting** toolbar (Fig 42) (or **Ctrl+Shift+S**).

Fig 42

Click **Format**, **Style** from the menu bar.
This will display the **Styles** dialogue box (Fig 43).

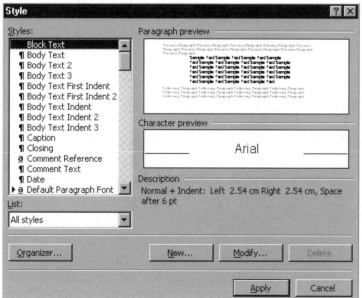

Select **All styles** from the **List:** drop-down box.

Click on each style in the **Styles:** list to display a **Preview** on the right.

A **Character preview** will also be displayed, together with a **Description**, indicating the make up of the style selected, ie the font, size and any paragraph formatting, if used.

Fig 43

Types Of Style

Paragraph Styles

A paragraph style controls all aspects of a paragraph's appearance, such as text alignment, tab stops, line spacing and borders and can include character formatting. If you want a paragraph to have a particular combination of attributes that aren't in an existing style (for example, a bold, italic, centre-aligned heading in the Arial Narrow font), you can create a new paragraph style.

Character Styles

A character style affects selected text within a paragraph, such as the font and size of text and bold and italic formats. Characters within a paragraph can have their own style even if a paragraph style is applied to the paragraph as a whole. If you want to be able to give certain types of words or phrases the same kind of formatting and the formatting is not in an existing style, you can create a new character style.

Applying Existing Styles To Text

An existing style can be applied to a single paragraph or to groups of paragraphs, provided they have been selected. Styles can also be applied to characters such as single words or phrases within a paragraph.

To apply an existing style to a paragraph(s):

1.	Select or click into the paragraph(s).

2.	Click **Format**, **Style** from the menu bar.

3.	Select the style required from those available.

4.	Click **Apply**.

Alternatively, select a style from those available from the **Style** box on the formatting toolbar (Fig 42).

TASK

1.	*Open the document called **Meeting** for editing.*

2.	*Apply the 'Body Text Indent 2' style to the first and last paragraph.*

3.	*Apply the 'Body Text First Indent 2' style to the remaining paragraphs.*

4.	*Print preview the document and save the changes.*

To apply an existing style to a character(s):

1. Select or click into the character(s).

2. Click **Format**, **Style** from the menu bar.

3. Select the style required from those available.

4. Click **Apply**.

T A S K

1. *Highlight the text 'I.T. Department' within the paragraph headed 'Computers' and apply the **Emphasis** style.*

2. *Save the changes.*

Creating A New Style

Creating a new paragraph style

To create a new paragraph style, format an existing paragraph, incorporating all text enhancement required, together with any border and shading formatting.

With the paragraph selected, click into the **Styles** box on the formatting toolbar.

This will highlight the existing style name.

Type in a new name for the new **Style** and press the **Enter** key on the keyboard. The new style will now appear in the drop-down list.

Creating A New Character Style

To create a new character style, click **Format**, **Style** from the menu bar.

This will display the **Style** dialogue box (Fig 43).

Click **New**. This will display the **New Style** dialogue box (Fig 44).

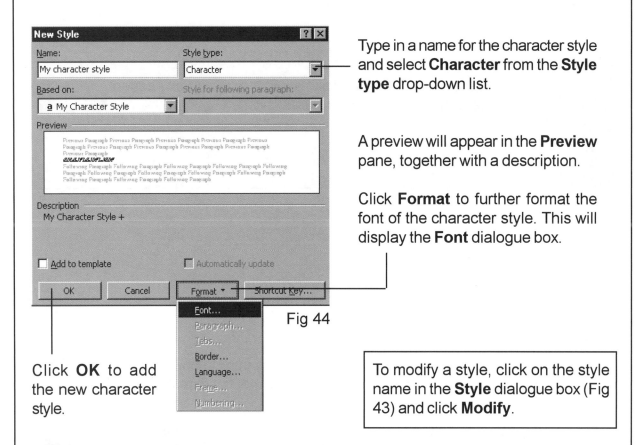

Type in a name for the character style and select **Character** from the **Style type** drop-down list.

A preview will appear in the **Preview** pane, together with a description.

Click **Format** to further format the font of the character style. This will display the **Font** dialogue box.

Fig 44

Click **OK** to add the new character style.

To modify a style, click on the style name in the **Style** dialogue box (Fig 43) and click **Modify**.

T A S K

1. Create a new character style called **Custom Style** comprising the following:

   Arial, size 20pt, blue, bold and shadow.

2. Apply the new style to the main heading in the document.

3. Create a new paragraph style called **Custom Para** comprising the following:

   Tahoma, size 12pt, based on 'Body Text' with the 'Caption' style.

4. Apply the new paragraph style to the last paragraph in the document.

5. Save the changes and preview the document.

6. Print the document and close.

Text Placement

Cutting, Copying And Pasting Within A Document

Three useful tools within any of the Microsoft Office 2000 applications are **Cut**, **Copy** and **Paste**. Within Word 2000 they are used to move and copy text within and between documents.

✂	**Cut** (**Ctrl+X**)	-	To move a selected piece of text from one location to another.
🖹	**Copy** (**Ctrl+C**)	-	To duplicate a selected piece of text to create a copy.
📋	**Paste** (**Ctrl+V**)	-	To complete either of the above actions.

Cut, copy and paste are available on the standard toolbar and the buttons are as above.

The standard procedure for cutting and copying

1. Select the text.
2. Click either **Cut** (move) or **Copy** (duplicate).
3. The selected text is placed on the **clipboard***.
4. Select the required location and click on **Paste**.

The **Cut**, **Copy** and **Paste** commands are also available from the menu bar by selecting **Edit** (Fig 45).

 ***The clipboard**

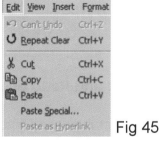

Fig 45

The clipboard is an area of temporary memory which will hold data, whether cut or copied, for it to be pasted elsewhere.

When an item is copied, the original will stay in its original position and a copy will be placed on the clipboard.

The clipboard is common to all Microsoft Office applications, therefore data can be cut or copied from one document to another or from one application to another.

When a piece of data has been cut or copied to the clipboard, it will remain there until the clipboard is full or the computer is switched off.

Cutting, Copying And Pasting Between Documents

To use cut, copy and paste between documents:

1.   Open or view the document from where the text is to be cut or copied.

2.   Select the text and click **Cut** or **Copy**.

3.   Open or view the document where the text is to be pasted (cut or copied to).

4.   Position the cursor and click **Paste**.

5.   Close any active or open documents which are no longer required.

Deleting Text

Deleting text using the keyboard

When editing a document, it may be necessary to delete selected parts of the text. This could be characters, words, sentences, paragraphs or complete sections of text.

Use the selecting or highlighting procedure to indicate which piece of text is to be deleted.

To delete, either use the **Delete** key or the **Backspace** key on the keyboard.

To delete text and replace it with new text, select/highlight it and type. The original text will be replaced as you type.

Using the Undo and Redo buttons

If you make a mistake at any time, use the **Undo** button on the standard toolbar to undo your last action.

Click on the **Undo** button (or **Ctrl+Z**).

To select a previous action to undo, click on the drop-down arrow (Fig 46) to view the actions you have carried out. Select the actions to undo by clicking on them.

Fig 46

To redo an action click on the redo button to repeat (or **Ctrl+Y**).

TASK

1. Create a template based on the **Professional Report** template. Replace the existing company name and address with the following:

> **Outsource Limited, 10-11 Vernon Way, Winchester, Lancashire, WH7 9LK. Tel: 01485 1166542 Fax: 01485 1166545**

2. Replace the title cover text with **Workshop Plan**.

3. Use page setup to set the following criteria:
A4-sized paper, portrait orientation, all margin measurements to 3cm. Apply these settings to the whole document.

4. Delete all text from subtitle cover 'Blue Sky's Best…' onwards and save the template as **Workshop_temp** to a new folder called **Plans** on your floppy disk. Close the template.

5. Create a new document based on the **Workshop_temp** template previously created.

6. Position the cursor beneath the heading 'Workshop Plan' and add the text **Health and Safety Workshop**. Format the text to Arial, size 20pt and bold. The heading may appear indented due to previously set formatting within the template. Remove the indentation.

7. Copy and paste the paragraph of text relating to Health and Safety from the document called **Meeting** and position below the heading 'Health and Safety Workshop'.

8. Delete the sentences beginning: 'Safety workshops…', 'Information will…' and 'All staff are to read…'

9. Format the paragraph to Arial, size 12pt.

10. Add the following text below the paragraph beginning 'All members…'

11. Format the heading of the list to a suitable style.

12. Add a header to contain the company name, aligned right.

13. Add a footer to contain the document name (left) and the date (right).

14. Save the document as **HSWorkshopPlan**, print page 1 only and close.

Workshop Content

The Health and Safety at Work Act (HSAWA)
Personal Safety Equipment
Movement of Trucks and Vehicles
Movement of Pedestrians
Lifting Heavy Items
Fire
Electricity
Daily Life
The Environment
Work Equipment
Hazardous Products
Working at Height
Medical Attention for Casualties

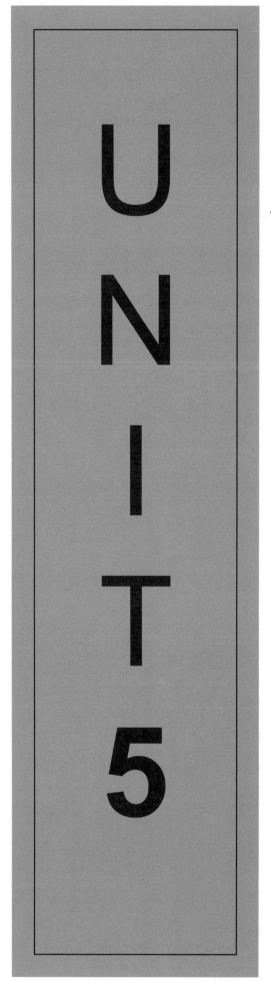

On completion of this unit, you will have learnt about and practised the following:

- **Checking Documents For Accuracy**

  - Document Checking
  - Checking Spelling
  - Adding New Words To A Dictionary
  - The Limitations Of Spell Checkers
  - Checking Grammar
  - Language
  - Thesaurus
  - Creating A Personal Dictionary
  - Editing A Personal Dictionary

©Tektra TEKWP2RP1102

Checking Documents For Accuracy

Document Checking

Once you have completed a document, it is important to perform certain checks to ensure that it is free from errors. Using a spell checker can quickly eliminate any spelling errors electronically. However, it will not pick up certain errors of typing, such as typing 'you' instead of 'your'. The spell checker recognises both of these words as correct, therefore your document will need to be proofread manually to check the meaning of words in sentences. Check documents for accuracy of information and correctness where possible.

Final checks should include the following:

- Spell checking (against the correct language)
- Grammar checking
- Correctness of information and meanings
- Printed outcome (print preview for accuracy and layout)

Checking Spelling

All word processed documents should be checked for spelling errors. This is sometimes known as 'proofing'. Word 2000 has a facility to do just this and checks each word in your document against a standard dictionary. If a word is unknown to the dictionary, it will be 'flagged' by the appearance of a red wavy line underneath the word (if this feature is activated).

Either check the whole document or a selection which has been highlighted. If checking the whole document, ensure the cursor is appearing at the top (beginning) of the document or the check will commence from where the cursor is positioned.

To activate the spell checker, either use the button on the standard toolbar

or press **F7**

or select **Tools**, **Spelling and Grammar** from the menu bar.

The **Spelling and Grammar** dialogue box will be displayed (Fig 47).

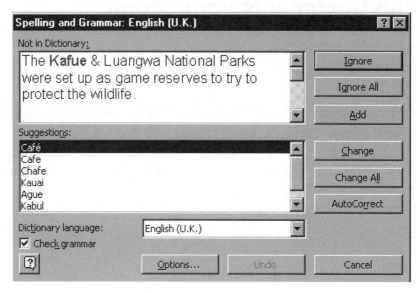

Fig 47

Notice the **Not in Dictionary** box in Fig 47 is displaying the unrecognised word in red, together with a suggestion in the box below.

The buttons on the right of the dialogue box are:

Ignore	-	Skips the highlighted word without making changes
Ignore All	-	Skips over all occurrences of the word without making changes
Add	-	Adds the highlighted word to the dictionary
Change	-	Replaces the original word with a chosen suggestion
Change All	-	Replaces all occurrences of the word with a chosen suggestion
AutoCorrect	-	Adds a misspelled word and its correction to the AutoCorrect list; future misspelling of the word will be automatically corrected

To proceed to check the document, one of the above buttons must be selected for the checker to move onto the next word.

The spell checker may not recognise the names of people or places. When working from home or in the office, if words are used regularly, check them manually and then add to the dictionary if required.

Once the spell checker reaches the end of the document, it will display a message (Fig 48). Click **OK**.

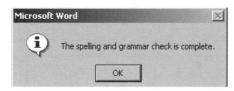

Fig 48

Adding New Words To A Dictionary

If you are a regular user of a word processor such as Microsoft Word you may at times come across certain words that are specific to yourself and not contained within the standard dictionary that Word will check against. This can also be the case where you insert large amounts of text about a specialist subject such as medicine or archaeology.

To eliminate having to manually check those words every time they are typed into a document, enter the correct spelling and **Add** them to the dictionary when they are flagged by the spell checker. In future, when the words are typed correctly the spell checker will not flag them.

Names of people and places will almost always be flagged by a spell checker, as they are not words that would normally appear in a standard dictionary. Either manually check them or add them to your dictionary accordingly.

The Limitations Of Spell Checkers

Even though it may seem tempting to rely on a spell checker to correct all spelling mistakes in a document, this is not always recommended.

The spell checker cannot always check for the correct meaning of a word or that the correct word has been used. The grammar checker may pick up these instances. However, as with the spelling checker, this cannot be relied upon.

For example, look at the following sentences; are there any spelling mistakes?

All attendees of the meeting picked up there minutes and left the room.

Please leave you bags outside of the Meeting room.

Before starting, have our supplementary pages ready to read.

There are no spelling mistakes, but the incorrect words have been used as follows:

All attendees of the meeting picked up **their** minutes and left the room.

Please leave **your** bags outside of the Meeting room.

Before starting, have **your** supplementary pages ready to read.

The spell checker has not picked up the mistakes, so a manual proofread of the document is recommended, where these types of error can be highlighted and corrected before printing.

Checking Grammar

Microsoft Word 2000 will check the grammar of the text in a document and, if the feature has been activated, will display possible grammatical problems with a green wavy line appearing underneath them.

To perform a grammar check, either select the tool on the standard toolbar or click on **Tools**, **Spelling and Grammar** from the menu bar. Notice the small check box appearing at the bottom of the dialogue box to check the grammar.

When the checker reaches a grammar problem, it will be highlighted in green, together with suggestions on how to correct the problem. Choose again from the buttons appearing on the right of the dialogue box.

Be aware when checking for spelling and grammar: it cannot check for every eventuality!

If the computer you are using does not display the red and green wavy lines underneath misspelled words and grammatical problems select **Tools**, **Options**, **Spelling & Grammar** from the menu bar. In the spelling section, ensure the box is checked to 'Check spelling as you type' and 'Check grammar as you type' in the **Grammar** section. Click **OK** to activate.

TASK

1.   *Open the document called **Draft Report** and print.*

2.   *Check the document for spelling and grammar errors and correct any found.*

3.   *Check the overall document for layout, correct any formatting which may appear inappropriate and indicate the sections changed in writing on the printout.*

4.   *Save the document as **Final Report** and close.*

Language

When you use the spell checker, it compares the words in your document with those in its main dictionary. The main dictionary contains most common words, but it might not include proper names, technical terms, acronyms and so on. To prevent the spell checker from questioning such words, you can add the words to a custom dictionary. Microsoft Word provides a built-in custom dictionary, but you can also create your own (customised dictionary).

The **Custom Dictionary** will be assigned a language; this will be dependant on which options were selected at the time the application was installed. There are many languages available in Word 2000.

To check which language is being used, either check the **status** bar (the current language will be displayed):

| REC | TRK | EXT | OVR | English (U.K | 📖 |

or

select **Tools**, **Language**, **Set Language** from the menu bar to activate the **Language** dialogue box and change if required.

Select the language required and the spell checker and other tools will automatically check documents using this language.

Thesaurus

A thesaurus is a dictionary of synonyms (a word or phrase meaning the same as another in the same language). Word 2000 contains a built-in Thesaurus which will look up words and phrases and replace them with alternatives.

Click **Tools**, **Language**, **Thesaurus** to activate the **Thesaurus** dialogue box (Fig 49) (or **Shift+F7**).

Ensure the thesaurus is checking against the correct language (this will appear on the title bar of the dialogue box).

The word looked up in this example is 'Training'.

The meaning of the word will appear below, together with a list of suggested alternatives (synonyms) on the right.

To select an alternative, click on the word and click on **Replace**.

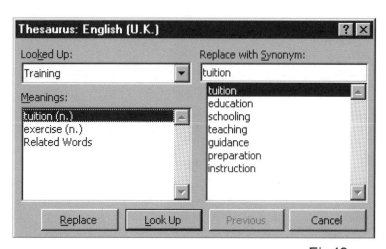

Fig49

T A S K

1. Using the document **Final Report**, check that the language being used is **English (U.K.)**.

2. Use the thesaurus to replace the following words and phrases in the document:

   findings *(1st paragraph)*
   speaker *(2nd paragraph)*
   caused by *(4th paragraph)*

3. Save the changes to the document and close.

©Tektra TEKWP2RP1102

Creating A Personal Dictionary

When checking words using the spell checker in Word 2000, it will check words against the standard 'Custom dictionary'. This is a file called Custom.dic. It contains words the same as a normal paper-based dictionary would.

A personal dictionary is used when you have specific words which will appear in your documents, but which do not need to be added to the main dictionary, such as words relating to specific names or places or specialised subjects, like the medical profession.

To create a new personal dictionary, click **Tools**, **Options** and select the **Spelling and Grammar** tab.

Click on the **Dictionaries** button. This will display the **Custom Dictionaries** dialogue box (Fig 50).

Click **New**. ————————————

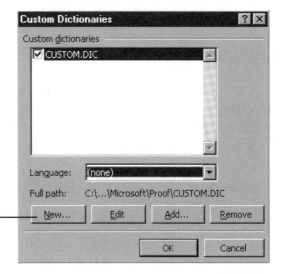

Fig 50

This will display the **Create Custom Dictionary** dialogue box (Fig 51), which requires a location and name for your personal dictionary.

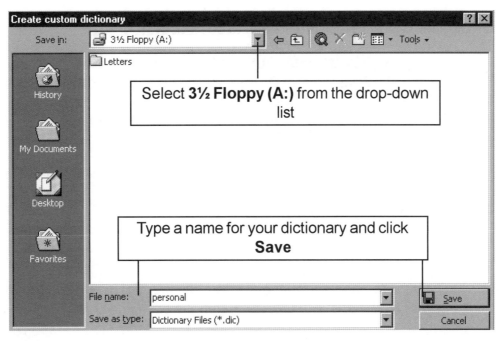

Fig 51

The **Custom Dictionaries** dialogue box will now display two dictionaries, the Custom one and your personal one.

Ensure there is a tick in each check box and
Click **OK**.

The spell checker will now check all words in a document against both dictionaries if the tick appears in both check boxes.

Your personal dictionary is ready to be edited, ie for words to be added to it. These can be names of people or places etc.

Editing A Personal Dictionary

To add words to your personal dictionary, click on the **Dictionaries** button from the **Spelling and Grammar** tab.

Click on the name of your personal dictionary and click on the **Edit** button.

A message will be displayed explaining that when a dictionary is edited, it will stop the automatic spell checking facility from working. Click **OK** to proceed.

> **Microsoft Word**
>
> ⚠ Word stops automatic spell checking when you edit a dictionary. To restart after you close the dictionary, choose Tools / Options / Spelling and Grammar tab and select the Check Spelling As You Type check box.
>
> [OK]   [Cancel]

This will open your dictionary as a **Word** document.

Type in the words required and click **File**, **Save** then **File**, **Close**.

This will return you to your document.

The automatic spell checking facility will need to be re-activated.

Select **Tools**, **Options** from the menu bar and click on the **Spelling and Grammar** tab. Place a tick in the 'Check spelling as you type' option and click **OK**.

T A S K		
	1.	Open the document **Harvard Letter**.
	2.	Create a personal dictionary on your floppy disk and call it **Suppliers**.
	3.	Add the following words to the dictionary:
		Harvard; **Inkleys**; **Hickories**; **Lonintons**
	4.	Spell check the document against both the custom dictionary and the Suppliers dictionary. Ensure the automatic spell check facility is re-activated.
	5.	Save the changes to the document and close.

CONSOLIDATION EXERCISE

You have been asked to produce a report for your supervisor, the content of which is detailed below.

1. *Create a new document and set to portrait orientation with margins of top and bottom - 2.5cm, left and right - 3cm. Use Arial 12pt.*

2. *Add a header to the document to include the date and page number. The date should be aligned left and the page number aligned right.*

3. *Add a footer to include the filename.*

4. *Type in the text below:*

2002 Company Report

New Offices

The opening of the new office will go ahead as planned this month, with approximately 30 Staff being relocated to the new office. A letter is being sent to those members of staff affected by the move and a meeting has been arranged to brief them on the new office layout.

New Workshops

New workshops are to commence in April after a marketing questionnaire found that there is a demand for them. Workshops will include 'Psychology in the Workplace' and 'A Guide to Good Management'. Stuart Riddings will take the workshops with a view to introducing another member of staff later in the year. The new workshops will take place in the following towns: Marlena, Wyvale, Petersborough and Singford.

New Staff

New staff are to be employed in the latter part of the year following a demand for the Motivation Workshops. We shall also be introducing a new style of 'Road Show Workshops', taking them out into business environments and tailoring them to suit the needs of Companies.

5. *Format the main heading '2002 Company Report' with the style **Heading 1**.*

6. *Create a new style and call it **Sub-style**. The style should be Arial, size 14pt, bold and blue. Format all sub-headings to the new style.*

7. *Format the alignment of all paragraphs to fully justified.*

8. *Copy and paste the company name only from the letter template 'Outsource_temp' and insert at the top of the report.*

C O N S O L I D A T I O N   E X E R C I S E

9. Create a personal dictionary on your floppy disk and call it
    My_dictionary.

    Add the following words to the dictionary:

    Marlena
    Wyvale
    Petersborough
    Singford

10. Check the document and ensure that you include checks for spelling
    (using both the custom dictionary and your personal dictionary) and
    grammar.   Ensure the check is carried out using the English (U.K.)
    language.   Use print preview to check the overall layout of the document.

11. Use the Thesaurus to replace the following words, ensuring that they are
    used in the correct context:

    brief (paragraph 1)
    include (paragraph 2)
    latter (paragraph 3)

12. Save the document as **Outsource Report 2002**.

13. Print the document.

14. Close the document.

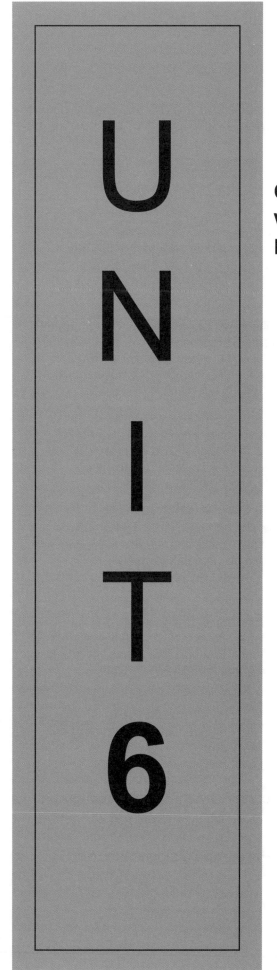

On completion of this unit, you will have learnt about and practised the following:

- **Working With Paragraphs**

  - Indents
  - Line Spacing
  - Spacing Before And After

- **Bulleted And Numbered Lists**

  - Bulleted Lists
  - Numbered Lists
  - Formatting Bulleted And Numbered Lists
  - Formatting Bulleted Lists
  - Formatting Numbered Lists

Working With Paragraphs

Indents

Indentation can be set for individual or multiple paragraphs and lines of text. It is the distance between the left and right edges of the text from the margin. Refer to Fig 52 below for examples of types of indentation:

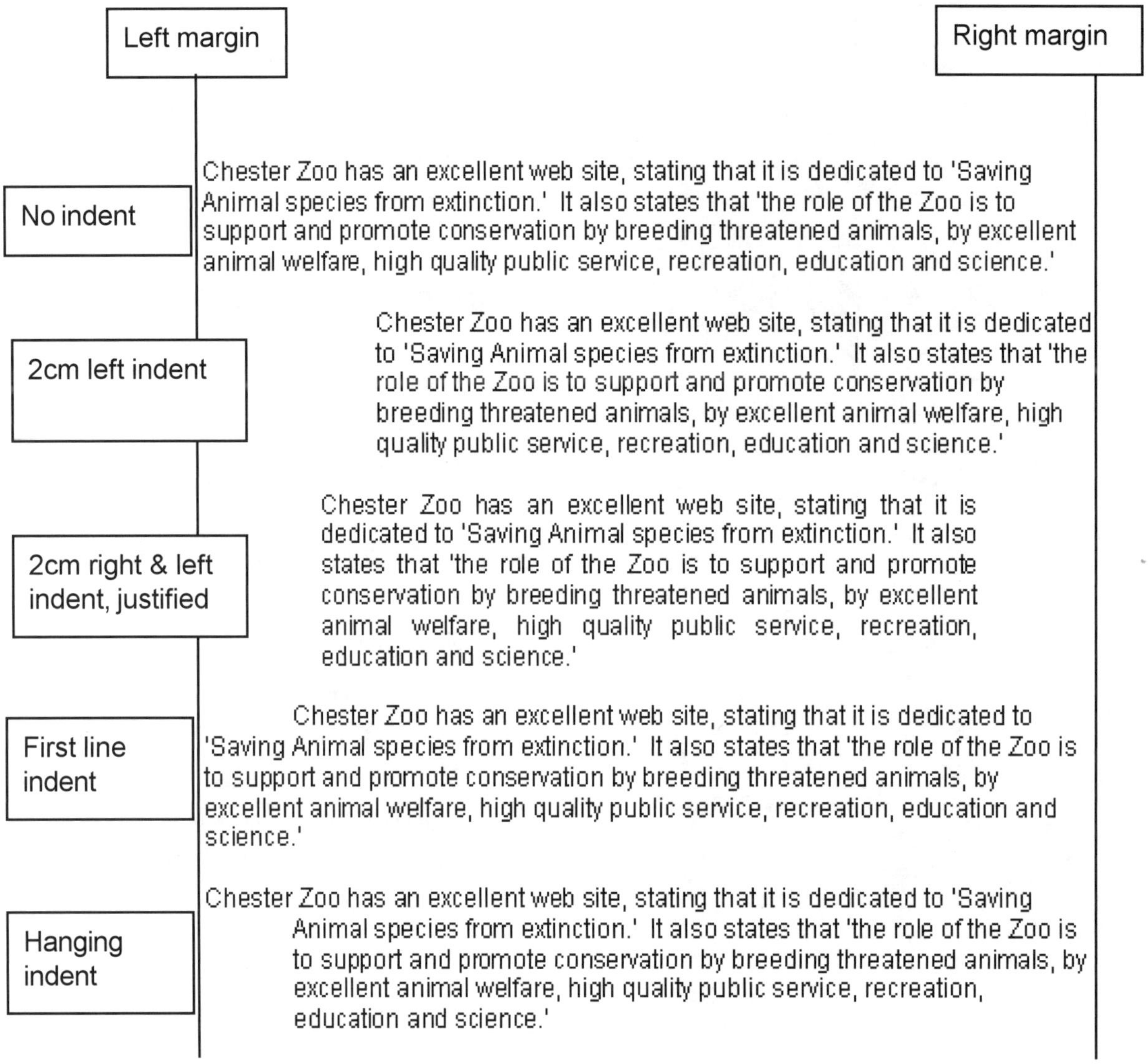

Left margin

Right margin

No indent

Chester Zoo has an excellent web site, stating that it is dedicated to 'Saving Animal species from extinction.' It also states that 'the role of the Zoo is to support and promote conservation by breeding threatened animals, by excellent animal welfare, high quality public service, recreation, education and science.'

2cm left indent

Chester Zoo has an excellent web site, stating that it is dedicated to 'Saving Animal species from extinction.' It also states that 'the role of the Zoo is to support and promote conservation by breeding threatened animals, by excellent animal welfare, high quality public service, recreation, education and science.'

2cm right & left indent, justified

Chester Zoo has an excellent web site, stating that it is dedicated to 'Saving Animal species from extinction.' It also states that 'the role of the Zoo is to support and promote conservation by breeding threatened animals, by excellent animal welfare, high quality public service, recreation, education and science.'

First line indent

Chester Zoo has an excellent web site, stating that it is dedicated to 'Saving Animal species from extinction.' It also states that 'the role of the Zoo is to support and promote conservation by breeding threatened animals, by excellent animal welfare, high quality public service, recreation, education and science.'

Hanging indent

Chester Zoo has an excellent web site, stating that it is dedicated to 'Saving Animal species from extinction.' It also states that 'the role of the Zoo is to support and promote conservation by breeding threatened animals, by excellent animal welfare, high quality public service, recreation, education and science.'

Fig 52

To apply indentation to a paragraph, position the cursor anywhere in the paragraph. To apply to more than one, select the paragraphs.

Select **Format**, **Paragraph**. This will display the **Paragraph** dialogue box (Fig 53).

Ensure the **Indents and Spacing** tab is selected.

Fig 53 The **Paragraph** dialogue box:

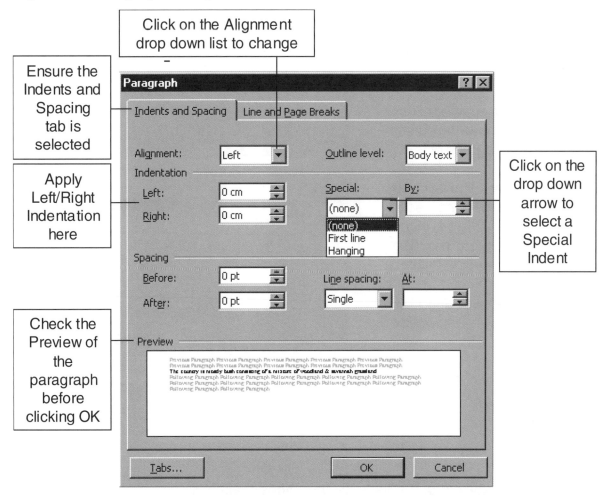

Click on the Alignment drop down list to change

Ensure the Indents and Spacing tab is selected

Apply Left/Right Indentation here

Click on the drop down arrow to select a Special Indent

Check the Preview of the paragraph before clicking OK

T A S K

1. *Open the document called **Meeting** for editing.*

2. *Add the text below as new paragraphs at the end of the document:*

Workshop Plans

All workshop plans are to be produced by the Sales department from this point forward. Any member of staff proposing an amendment to a plan should seek permission from a Supervisor.

Workshop plans will be kept in an orderly fashion and filed in alphabetical order. Any client wishing to receive a plan will be sent a Company Brochure, together with a brief introduction to the workshop in question.

The new Company Website will be launched this month. The Web address is www.outsourceworkshops.co.uk. Any member of staff wishing to add information to the website should inform the I.T. Department. All suggestions will be passed onto a Directors' meeting.

---

3. *Format the sub-title of the paragraph to Arial, size 14pt in bold.*

4. *Save the changes to the document.*

Line Spacing

Line spacing is the measurement of vertical space between lines of text. When a new document is created from the normal template, Word will automatically use single line spacing.

To format the line spacing of text in a document, move the cursor to the line or paragraph of text.

Select **Format**, **Paragraph** from the menu bar and notice the **Spacing** section (Fig 54) of the **Paragraph** dialogue box (Fig 53):

To change the line spacing, click on the drop-down arrow and select an option.

Click **OK** to apply or **Cancel** to abandon.

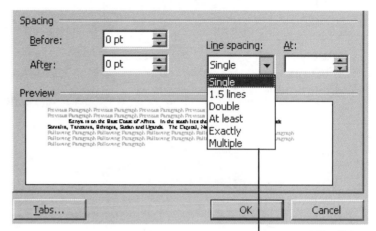

Fig 54

Refer to the table below for the line spacing options available:

Single	Line spacing for each line that allows for the largest font in that line and a small amount of extra space in addition.
1.5 Lines	Line spacing for each line that is 1½ times that of single line spacing.
Double	Line spacing for each line that is 2 times that of single line spacing.
At Least	Minimum line spacing that Word can adjust to allow for larger font sizes or graphics that would not otherwise fit.
Exactly	Fixed line spacing that Word does not adjust. All lines are evenly spaced using this option.
Multiple	Line spacing that is increased or decreased by a percentage specified by you. For example, setting a line spacing to a multiple of 1.2 will increase the space by 20% (percent). In the At box, type or select the line spacing required (the default is 3 lines).
At	The amount of line spacing selected. The option is only available when selecting At Least, Exactly or Multiple.

Spacing Before And After

Spacing before and after is used when additional spacing is required before and/or after a paragraph. In the example below (Fig 55), the second paragraph of text has had spacing applied before and after.

12pt
spacing
before ——————————

18pt
spacing ——————————
after

Line spacing determines the amount of vertical space between lines of text. Microsoft Word uses single line spacing by default.

The line spacing you select will affect all lines of text in the selected paragraph or in the paragraph that contains the insertion point. You set line spacing on the **Indents and Spacing** tab.

It a line contains a large text character, graphic or formula, Word increases the spacing for that line.

Fig 55

To apply spacing before or after, click into the paragraph or select multiple paragraphs as required and select **Format**, **Paragraph** from the menu bar.

This will display the **Paragraph** dialogue box (Fig 53).

Locate the **Spacing** section and enter the required spacing in the **Before** or **After** boxes (Fig 56).

Click **OK**.

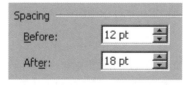

Fig 56

T A S K

1. *Using the document **Meeting**, apply a left and right indent of 2.5cm to the three paragraphs at the end of the document; fully justify the paragraphs.*

2. *Apply spacing **Before** and spacing **After** of 12pt to the last paragraph.*

3. *Apply the **Emphasis** style to the text I.T. Department.*

4. *Check the first paragraph and remove spacing before or after (if any).*

5. *Change double-line spacing in the first paragraph to single.*

6. *Ensure all paragraphs are fully justified throughout the document.*

7. *Save changes to the document.*

8. *Print the document and close.*

Bulleted And Numbered Lists

Bulleted Lists

Bulleted lists are used to list information. Numbered lists are used to list information which require a particular order. A **Bullet** tool and a **Numbering** tool appear on the formatting toolbar. Bullets and numbers can then be formatted in various styles.

 Bullets button (or Ctrl+Shift+L)

To apply bullets to an existing list, select the list and click on the **Bullets** button.

The buttons work as on and off switches. To remove bullet points from a list, select the list and click on the **Bullets** button.

Numbered Lists

Numbered lists are used to format a list of items, procedures or instructions in number format. By using the automatic numbering tool, numbers will appear consistent and in the same style.

To apply numbers to an existing list, select or highlight the list and click on the **Numbering** button.

 Numbering button

To activate bullets or numbering before entering the list of information, click on the button required and then type. When pressing the **Enter** key, either another bullet will appear on the next line or the next number in the list, depending on which button was selected.

Formatting Bulleted And Numbered Lists

When applying bullets or numbers to a list in a document, Word 2000 will insert the 'default' bullet point design or the 'default' number style. Your document may follow a particular design or layout which requires the bullets or numbers to be in a different format or design.

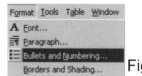

Fig 57

Select the list and click **Format**, **Bullets and Numbering** (Fig 57) from the menu bar. This will display the **Bullets and Numbering** dialogue box (Fig 58):

Formatting Bulleted Lists

Click on the **Bulleted** tab.

Click on the style of bullet required and a blue border will appear around the edge, click **OK**.

Click **Cancel** to abandon.

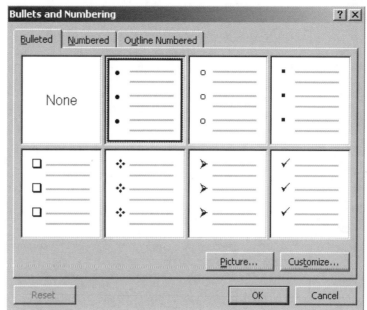

Fig 58

Click on the **Picture** button to reveal the **Picture Bullet** dialogue box (Fig 59).

A selection of alternative bullet points can be selected using this feature.

To select one, click on the bullet point design and a sub-menu will appear.

Click on the **Insert Clip** button to apply the bullet design to a list.

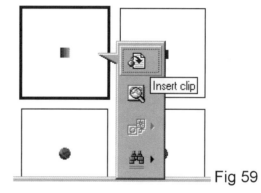

Fig 59

Click on the **Customize** button to reveal the **Customize Bulleted List** dialogue box (Fig 60). Here you can pinpoint an exact position for both bullet and text, see a preview and select symbols for a bullet by using the **Bullet** button.

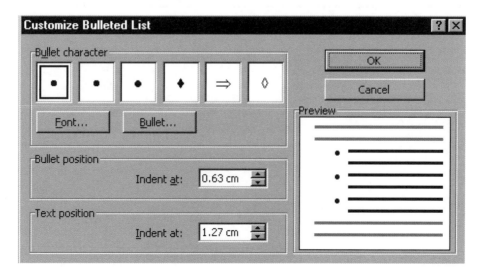

Fig 60

TASK

1. Open the document **HSWorkshopPlan**.

2. Apply bullet points to the Workshop Content List.

3. Format the bullet points to a picture of your choice.

4. Save the changes to the document.

5. Move the cursor to page 2 of the workshop plan. Ensure you are ready to add text at the top of page 2.

6. Add the following text:

Personal Safety Equipment

Accident Situations and Good Practice

Deep cuts – when handling sharp or pointed objects, wear suitable gloves.

Crushed toes – when handling objects, wear safety shoes. These will protect your toes if you drop anything.

Pieces of metal in the eye – when cutting or sawing, wear safety glasses, gloves and an apron.

Wood splinters – suitable gloves must be worn when handling objects likely to cause splinters or cuts.

---

7. Add a suitable style to the sub-titles 'Personal Safety Equipment' and 'Accident Situations and Good Practice'.

8. Apply bold to all text appearing before the dashes in the list.

9. Save the changes to the document.

Formatting Numbered Lists

Select the list and click **Format**, **Bullets and Numbering** from the menu bar. This will display the **Bullets and Numbering** dialogue box.

Click on the **Number** tab (Fig 61).

Click to select the required number format and a blue border will appear around the edge.

Click **OK** to apply the format or **Cancel** to abandon.

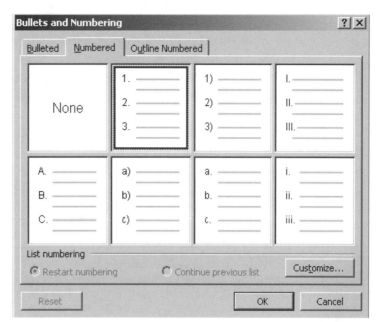

Fig 61

Applying Outline Numbering

Outline Numbering assigns a level to a piece of text or paragraph.

Click on the **Outline Numbered** tab (Fig 62).

Click to select the required number format and a blue border will appear around the edge.

Click **OK** to apply the format or **Cancel** to abandon.

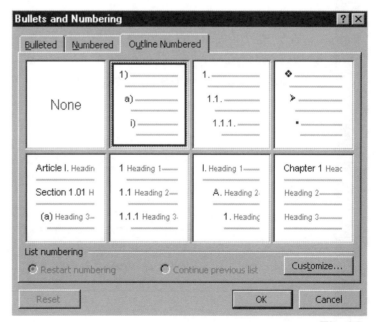

Fig 62

Word will automatically number items in a list when you press **Enter** at the end of a line.

For example, the first item in a list is typed starting with '1.' followed by the text. By pressing enter at the end of the line, Word will automatically enter the number '2.' for the next item. If the next item is on a different level, press the Tab key on the keyboard to display '1.1' for the next item, etc. Refer to the example in Fig 63.

Remember to use the Undo button if you make a mistake!

1. The movement of offices will go ahead as planned on 24 March 2002.

    1.1   The relocation plans will involve all staff.
    1.2   All desks are to be cleared by 23 March 2002.
    1.3   All equipment must be moved by 22 March 2002.

2. A Staff Induction will take place at the new offices on 26 March 2002.

    2.1   All Staff are to attend the Induction.
    2.2   The Induction will take place at 9.00am sharp.   Fig 63

T A S K

1. *Apply numbering to the list titled 'Accident Situations and Good Practice'.*

2. *Format the numbering of the above list to uppercase roman numerals eg I, II, III, IV.*

3. *Position the cursor on a new line below the numbered list and add the following text using outline numbering.*

> **Movement of Trucks and Vehicles**
>
> 1. **Possible Accident Situations**
>   a.   **Being hit by a lifting truck.**
>   b.   **Being hit by a truck wheel or tractor.**
>   c.   **Collisions – being hit by a vehicle.**
>
> 2. **Good Practice**
>   a.   **Do not ride on or be lifted by lifting trucks.**
>   b.   **Keep your distance from trucks at work or in motion.**
>   c.   **Never guide vehicles into position.**
>   d.   **Observe speed limits and traffic regulations in general.**

4. *Print page 2 only.*

5. *Save changes to the document.*

6. *Close the document.*

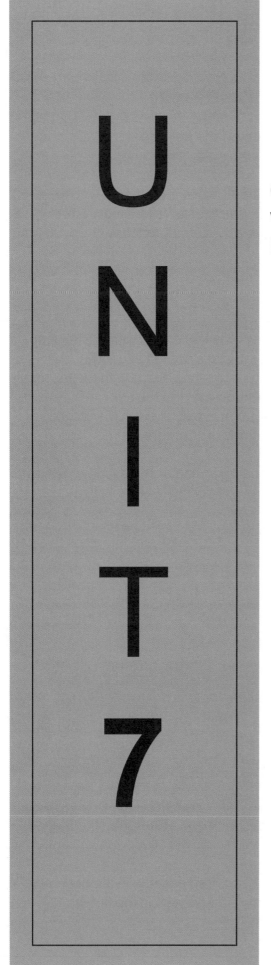

On completion of this unit, you will have learnt about and practised the following:

- **Working With Columns Of Data**

    - Tabs (Tabulation)
    - Adding Columns To A Document

Working With Columns Of Data

Tabs (Tabulation)

Tabs are used to control the vertical alignment of text in a document.

The default tab stops can be used (via the **Tab** key on the keyboard) or custom tab stops can be created which will override the default tab stops.

When the tab key is used on the keyboard, the tab stops are at increments of 1.27cm or 0.5 inches across the width of the page. The tab key is located on the left side of the keyboard, fourth button up, above the **Caps Lock** key. It has arrows pointing left and right on it.

The four most commonly used tabs are:

Left-aligned   -   The left edge of the text aligns with the tab stop.
                                             (The default tab stops are left aligned).
Right-aligned   -   The right edge of the text aligns with the tab stop.
Centre-aligned   -   The text is centred with the tab stop.
Decimal-aligned   -   The decimal point is aligned with the tab stop.
                                             Used for columns of numbers etc.

Fig 64 shows how markers will appear on the ruler bar to indicate which type of tab has been set.

Tab button (illustration shows decimal-aligned tab button).

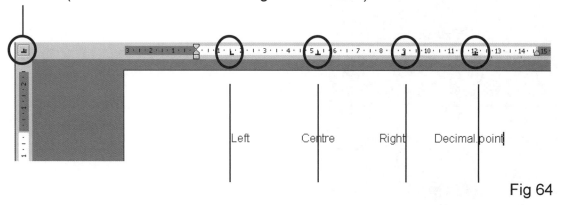

Fig 64

Tabs can be set by using the **Tab** button on the Ruler bar or by selecting **Format**, **Tabs** from the menu bar. If your ruler bar is not displayed, click **View**, **Ruler** from the menu bar.

To set tabs using the ruler, ensure the cursor is in the required position in the document. Click the tab button (see Fig 64) until the required tab is displayed on the button.

Using the mouse, click the position on the ruler bar (which is just below the measurement numbers on the ruler bar) where the tab is required.

Using the ruler bar is a quick way to set tabs. However, if you wish to be more accurate, select **Format**, **Tabs** from the menu bar. This will display the **Tabs** dialogue box (Fig 65).

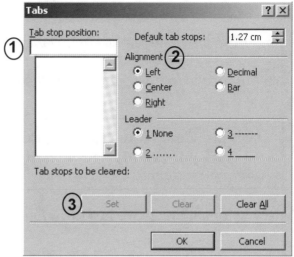

This dialogue box allows you to set all required tabs, and apply an alignment to them. Tabs can be cleared, if not required, by clicking on the **Clear** button or, to remove all tabs, click on **Clear All**.

Fig 65

To set a tab:

1.   Type in the measurement of the first tab in the **Tab stop position** box.

2.   Apply the required **Alignment**, Left, Centre, Right or Decimal.

3.   Click **Set**.

This will set the first tab stop position on the ruler bar.

If this is the only tab required, click **OK** to apply. If further tabs are required, type in the next tab stop position, apply an alignment and click **Set**. Repeat this process until all tabs are listed and click **OK**.

To reach the tab stop positions to commence typing, use the **Tab** key on the keyboard. The new tab stop positions created will override the existing default tab stops.

**T
A
S
K**

1. *Start a new blank document.*

2. *Add the title 'Workshop Schedule', centre it and format with a suitable style from those available.*

3. *Set the page with margins of 3cm all around (ie top, bottom, left and right).*

4. *Set the page orientation to landscape, sized for A4 paper.*

5. *Add the following text below the heading:*

This is the Workshop Schedule for the next month; this does not include new workshops.

---

6. *Format the above text to Tahoma, size 14pt, bold and centred.*

7. *Add the following text formatted to Tahoma, size 12pt. Set appropriate tab stop positions.*

Workshop	Tutor	Date	Time
A Guide to Good Management	J. Gibson	Apr 19	14.00 hrs
Communication in the Workplace	L. Harrison	Apr 22	13.00 hrs
Understanding Teamwork	R. Biggs	Apr 3	18.00 hrs
The Key to Motivating a Team	J. Kindred	Apr 6	15.00 hrs

8. *Add a header to the document to include the company name (right).*

9. *Add a footer to the document to include your name (left) and the date (right).*

10. *Save the document as **Workshop Schedule**.*

11. *Print the document.*

12. *Close the document.*

Adding Columns To A Document

If the type of document you are creating is a newsletter, flyer or brochure, you may find it necessary to make use of the **Columns** facility in Word 2000. Using columns will break up a normal document from the standard single column.

Fig 66 below is an example of a document created using three columns including a line in-between them.

MENU 1	MENU 2	MENU 3
Broccoli & Stilton Soup Prawn Cocktail Melon Extraordinaire	Onion Soup Prawn Toasts with Plum Sauce Sardine Salad	Sardine Salad Bread with Mixed Sushi Tuna & Mushroom Regatta
<O>	<O>	<O>
Chicken A-la-King Lamb with Courgettes Beef in red wine	Lasagne Verde Traditional Sunday Lunch Thick Country Soup Scotch Broth	8oz Steak in Pepper Sauce Beef Medley Lamb Medallions
Pasta with Wild Mushrooms Mixed Salad with Tuna		Pasta with Tomato & Basil Penne with Pesto & Salad
<O>	<O>	<O>
Italian Tiramisu Flaked Almond Bake Chocolate Nightmare	Sponge Surprise Flaky Choco Bread Ice-cream Devil's Cake	Nut Frenzy Ice-cream with Jelly Secret Flaky Bake

Fig 66

Columns added to a document in Word 2000 are 'Newspaper Columns', where the text flows to the bottom of one column and then flows onto the next.

There are alternatives to this method, which will depend on your requirements.

Before adding text to a document, consider the format, ie how many columns will be required, will the document be landscape or portrait and how much width should be allowed for each column.

To navigate between columns using the keyboard:

End of column   Alt+Pg Down
Start of column   Alt+Pg Up

To add columns to a document, click **Format**, **Columns** from the menu bar.

This will display the **Columns** dialogue box (Fig 67).

The box is split into sections: **Presets**, **Width and Spacing** and **Preview**.

Fig 67

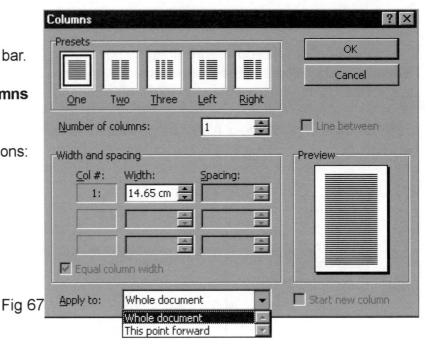

Presets

Select from the following;

One	This is a normal document, one column of data.
Two	The page will be split into two equal width columns.
Three	The page will be split into three equal width columns.
Left	Two unequal width columns, a wider column on the right.
Right	Two unequal width columns, a wider column on the left.

A page can be formatted to contain up to 11 columns on one page. Use the **Number of columns** box to enter the required amount.

Width and Spacing

The width and spacing section allows you to specify an exact measurement for the width of the columns and the spacing in between them.

Preview

Before clicking **OK** to confirm any changes, the **Preview** section will display the settings you have applied.

If they are incorrect, click **Cancel** to abandon the settings and try again.

Apply the column settings to the **Whole document** or **This point forward** using the **Apply to** box.

**T
A
S
K**

1. Start a new blank document.

2. Set the page to Landscape, A4 paper, and margins of:

   Top and bottom: 6 cm
   Left and right: 5 cm

3. Format the document to three equal columns with a line between each.

4. Add the following text to each column (you will need to press the **Enter** key many times to move from the bottom of the text in column one to the top of column two).

A Guide to Good Management	Communication in the Workplace	Understanding Teamwork
J. Gibson	L. Harrison	R. Biggs
Apr 19	Apr 22	Apr 3
14.00 hrs	13.00 hrs	18.00 hrs
4 Hours Places Limited	2 Hours Full	4 Hours Spaces Available

5. Format the text as shown, ie bold, centred, Arial, 14pt. You may need to tidy up the appearance after the text formatting.

6. Save the document as **Workshop Columns**.

7. Print the document.

8. Close the document.

C O N S O L I D A T I O N   E X E R C I S E

1. Open the document **Outsource Report 2002** for editing.

2. Apply a first line indent to the first paragraph.

3. Apply a hanging indent to the second paragraph.

4. Apply a left indent at 3cm to the third paragraph.

5. Type the sub-heading **'Agenda'** below the first paragraph.

6. Type the following agenda items and use outline numbering.

1	**Office Layout**
1.1	**Desks**
1.2	**Computers**
1.3	**Facilities**
2	**Departments**
2.1	**Office Space**
2.2	**Equipment**
2.3	**Conference Facilities**
3	**Recreation Area**
3.1	**Notice Boards**
3.2	**Responsibilities**
3.3	**Health and Safety**

7. Insert the following text below the second paragraph headed 'New Workshops'. Use appropriate tab stop positions.

Psychology in the Workplace	**Apr 9**	**Apr 11**	**Apr 16**	**9.00am**
A Guide to Good Management	**Apr 10**	**Apr 12**	**Apr 17**	**10.00am**

8. To the first paragraph apply spacing before of 5pt and spacing after of 6pt.

9. Save the changes to the report.

10. Check the report and view the layout in print preview.

11. Print the report and close.

On completion of this unit, you will have learnt about and practised the following:

- **Working With Breaks**

  - Page Breaks
  - Section Breaks
  - Column Breaks

Working With Breaks

Page Breaks

A Page Break is the point at which one page ends and another begins. There are two types of page break, **Automatic** (soft) and **Manual** (hard).

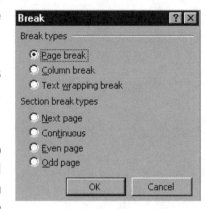

Fig 68

An automatic (soft) page break occurs automatically when a page is full with text or graphics, spilling further data onto another page.

A manual (hard) page break can be inserted to 'force' text or graphics onto a new page. A manual or hard page break can be inserted by clicking on **Insert**, **Break** on the menu bar. This will open the **Break** dialogue box (Fig 68).

Select **Page break** and click **OK** (or **Ctrl+Enter**).

A page break appears as a single horizontal dotted line (in normal view). The line is not visible in print layout view (unless the **Show/Hide** button is activated).

To remove a manual page break, move the cursor to the line containing the break and press delete (in normal view). To remove in print layout view, click on the **Show/Hide** button on the standard toolbar, click on the line containing the break and press delete.

When using a manual (hard) page break, all text after (below) the break will appear on the next page.

Fig 69 below is an example of break types displayed in normal view.

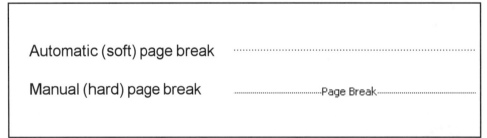

Fig 69

T		
A	1.	*Open the document called **Meeting** for editing.*
S	2.	*Insert a hard page break after the paragraph titled 'Conference Facilities'.*
K	3.	*Save the changes to the document.*

<u>Section Breaks</u>

Sections are used to vary the layout of a document, either within a page or between pages. Sections are inserted to divide the document so that different types of formatting can be applied between sections.

For example, the first section of a report may require a two column layout, the second section - appearing on the same page - may require a three column layout. By inserting section breaks between the two, this formatting can be applied.

Fig 70 below is an example of a document with sections applied. The document is split into three sections.

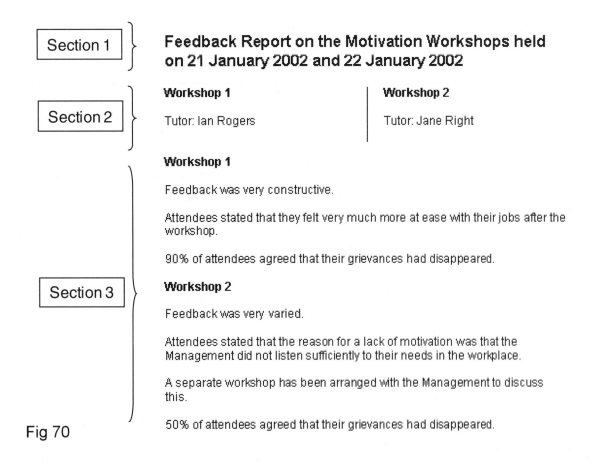

Fig 70

Section 1 contains the heading of the document; **Section 2** contains a two column layout and **Section 3** contains normal text.

Sections can be viewed more effectively in Normal View. The above is in Print Layout View.

Some of the different types of formatting which can be applied to different sections are margins, orientation (landscape or portrait), page borders, headers and footers, columns, page numbering, alignment and line numbering.

This is useful when your document has a mixture of requirements, ie a header page in portrait and the remaining pages in landscape.

To insert a **section break** select **Insert**, **Break** from the menu bar.

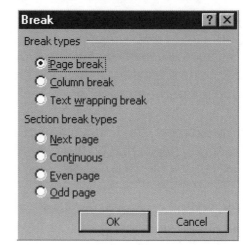

The **Break** dialogue box will appear (Fig 71).

There are four types of section break.

Select the break required and click on **OK**.

Fig 71

Next Page   A new section will appear at the top of the next page.

Continuous   The new section will begin on the same page (as per Fig 70).

**Odd or Even
Page**   The new section will begin on the next even or next odd page.

To delete a section break, view the document in Normal View and click on the section break (which will appear with a double line), then press **Delete**.

Alternatively, if inserting the break was your last action, remember you can use the **Undo** button to remove it!

Take care when deleting section breaks if there is already existing text held in that section; it will become part of the preceding section.

T A S K		
	1.	*Using the document **Meeting**, insert a **Next page** section break at the end of page 2.*
	2.	*View the document in normal view.*
	3.	*View the document in print layout view.*
	4.	*Save the changes to the document.*
	5.	*Close the document.*

Column Breaks

Column breaks are used to force text appearing in one column onto the next column.

In the examples below (Figs 72 and 73), there are two columns, Fig 72 is shown without a column break and Fig 73 is shown with a column break.

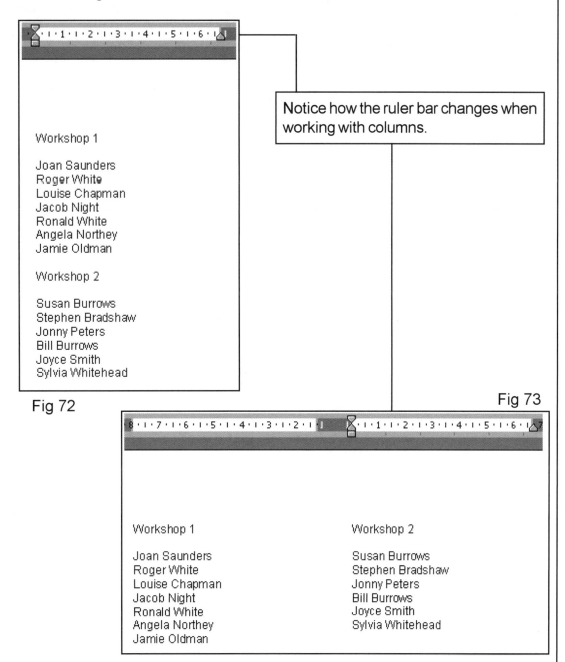

Notice how the ruler bar changes when working with columns.

Fig 72

Fig 73

To insert a column break, select **Insert**, **Break** from the menu bar, click **Column break** and click **OK** (or **Ctrl+Shift+Enter**).

To view any breaks that have been added to your document, use **View**, **Normal View**. Remember that breaks can be deleted by clicking on them in normal view and pressing **Delete**.

T A S K

1. Open the document called **Workshop Columns**.

2. Insert column breaks between the columns to ensure the text always appears in each column.

   NB The text will shift within the columns (due to the extra blank lines). Re-adjust the layout (delete blank lines) and ensure previously applied text formatting is correct.

3. View the document in normal view and notice the column breaks.

4. View the document in print layout view.

5. Save the changes to the document.

On completion of this unit, you will have learnt about and practised the following:

- **Additional Features**

    - Superscript And Subscript
    - Inserting Special Characters And Symbols

- **Find And Replace**

    - Finding Text In A Document
    - Replacing Text In A Document
    - Search Options

Additional Features

Superscript And Subscript

Superscript means to 'add text above', for example if in the text '24th January 1968' the 'th' is required to appear above the normal line of text as '24th January 1968'.

Subscript means to 'add text below', for example if in the text 'H20' (as in water) the '2' is required to appear below the normal line of text as H_2O.

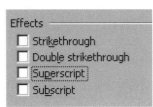

To apply either of the above to text, highlight the text and click **Format**, **Font** from the menu bar. The **Font** dialogue box will appear (or **Ctrl+D**).

Locate the **Effects** section of the box and click either the **Superscript** or **Subscript** boxes.

Alternatively, press **Ctrl+Shift+=** for superscript or **Ctrl+=** for subscript.

Click **OK**.

**T
A
S
K**

1. *Open the document called* **Meeting** *for editing.*

2. *Add the following text to page 3 of the document:*

   > **A Guide to Good Management
   > Communication in the Workplace
   > Understanding Teamwork**

   Format the text to Arial size 14. Ensure that there are no indents present and the spacing is set to single 6pt before and 6pt after.

3. *Add numbers to the end of the text to indicate footnotes which will be inserted later, formatting the numbers to be superscript.*

   > **A Guide to Good Management[1]
   > Communication in the Workplace[2]
   > Understanding Teamwork[3]**

4. *Save the changes to the document.*

5. *Print page 3 only and close the document.*

Inserting Special Characters And Symbols

Special characters and symbols may be required in a document such as the © (copyright) symbol or ½ (half) symbol. Other useful symbols include accents (a mark on the letter to show how it is pronounced), such as ê, é, è and à. As these characters and symbols are not available from the keyboard, Word 2000 has a facility to insert them into a document.

Click **Insert**, **Symbol** from the menu bar. This will display the **Symbol** dialogue box (Fig 74). Ensure the **Symbols** tab is selected.

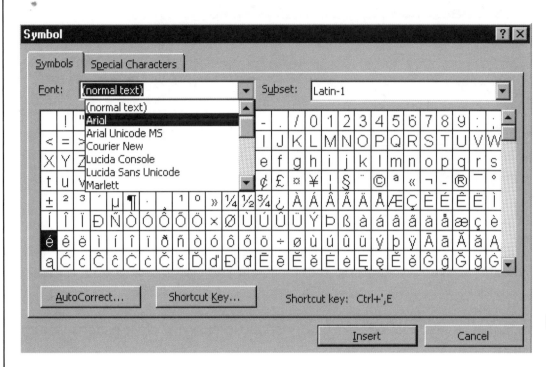

Fig 74

To use a symbol from those available, click on it and then on the **Insert** button. This will place it in your document at the position of the cursor.

The **Symbol** dialogue box will remain open for you to insert another if required. When ready to return to your document, click on the cross at the top right of the dialogue box.

Some of the most common font character sets used for symbols are:

Symbol	-	Greek letters, mathematical symbols, arrows, trademark and copyright symbols.
Normal Text	-	Accent letters, special marks, currency symbols, paragraph symbol.
Wingdings	-	Icons, envelopes, telephones, arrows, shapes, numbers etc.

If accents are required on letters, for example with the word 'rosé' the 'e' requires an accent, click **Insert**, **Symbol** and select the relevant font character set (such as Arial) from the drop-down list.

Locate the letter and select it. Click **Insert**.

Some special characters are classed as symbols and so may be found under both the 'Symbols' tab and 'Special Characters' tab. Examples of special characters are types of dash, space, hyphen and quote.

Click on **Insert**, **Symbol** from the menu bar and select the **Special Characters** tab (Fig 75):

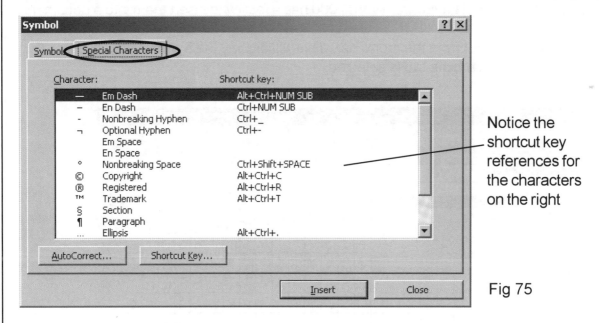

Notice the shortcut key references for the characters on the right

Fig 75

To insert any of the above into your document, click to select it and click on the **Insert** button.

When all special characters required have been inserted, click on the close button to return to your document.

Here is a description of some of the most regularly used special characters:

En dash	-	A dash that is the longer than the hyphen on the keyboard.
Em dash	-	Longer than an en dash, used between text for pauses and a change of thought.
En space	-	A slightly longer space than the normal one.
Em space	-	A slightly longer space than the en space.
Non-breaking space	-	A space which will not break at the end of a line. Words, names or dates separated by a non-breaking space will always stay on the same line.
Non-breaking hyphen	-	Two words separated by a non-breaking hyphen will always stay on the same line.

T
A
S
K

1. Edit the header of the document called **HSWorkshopPlan** and add the copyright symbol to appear at the beginning of the company name.

2. Add the following text at the end of the first paragraph:

> **These Workshops have been provided by Safetech™.**

3. Insert a symbol of a globe at the end of the heading 'Workshop Plan'. Use the Webdings character set.

4. Save the changes to the document.

5. Print the document.

6. Close the document.

Find And Replace

Finding Text In A Document

Using a tool to find or locate text within a document can be useful when working in larger documents. A common word which appears throughout a document may need enhancing (being made bold or underlined), and instead of manually looking through a complete document, the **Find** tool will search the document for you.

Fig 76

Find is a facility which will search a document for specified text (words, sentences and phrases for example). The whole document will be searched unless a specific section has been highlighted or selected.

To activate this tool and find text within a document, click **Edit**, **Find** from the menu bar (Fig 76) and the **Find and Replace** dialogue box (Fig 77) will be displayed (or **Ctrl+F**).

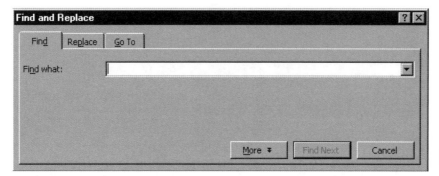

Fig 77

In the **Find what** box, type in the text you wish to locate in the document.

The **Find Next** button will be activated, click on this to begin the search.

If the matching text is found, the find facility will stop, however the dialogue box will remain open.

Edit the text as required when found and continue the search by clicking **Find Next** or, if the search is complete, click on the **close** button (cross) or press **Esc** on the keyboard.

Replacing Text In A Document

To find text and replace it, click **Edit**, **Replace** from the menu bar (or **Ctrl+H**).

The **Find and Replace** dialogue box (Fig 78) will appear, however this time, the **Replace** tab will be activated.

Fig 78

In the **Find what** box, type in the text you wish to replace (take care not to insert additional spaces).

In the **Replace with** box, type in the text to replace the existing text (take care not to insert additional spaces).

The **Find Next** box will become activated. Click on this to begin the search.

When the first occurrence of the text is found, either replace this one occurrence or replace all occurrences by clicking on the **Replace All** button.

Once complete, click on the **close** button (or cross).

Search Options

To intensify a find and replace, or a general search in a document, further options are available by clicking on the **More** button in the **Find and Replace** dialogue box. This will expand the box to reveal further search options (Fig 79).

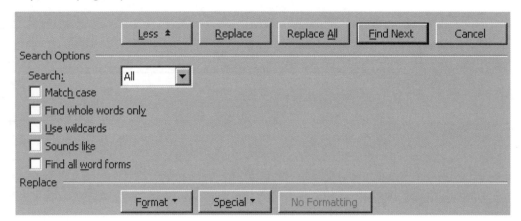

Fig 79

Search options include searching for words that match case, finding whole words only, using 'wildcards' (words that start or finish with certain characters and words which sound like others).

Clicking **Format** allows you to find or replace text with a specific **Format** (font, paragraph, language, style etc). Clicking **Special** allows you to find or replace specific commands or characters.

T A S K

1. *Open the document called **Meeting** for editing.*

2. *Find all occurrences of the word 'Supervisor' and replace them with the same word formatted to bold.*

3. *Find the text 'Health and Safety at Work Act' and format to italics.*

4. *Save the changes to the document.*

5. *Close the document.*

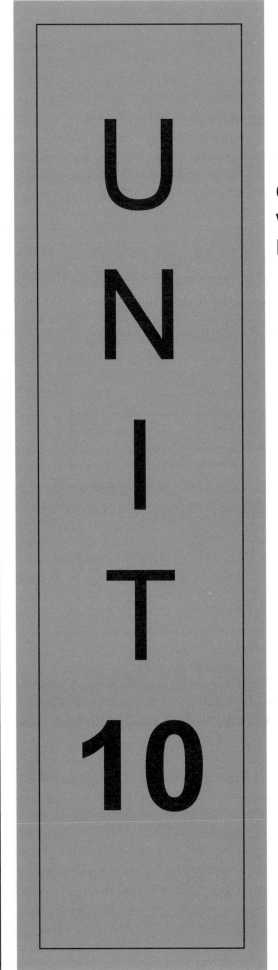

On completion of this unit, you will have learnt about and practised the following:

- **Producing A Mail Merge**

  - What Is A Mail Merge?
  - Common Uses Of A Mail Merge
  - Creating A Mail Merge
  - Creating A Data Source
  - Previewing Merged Documents
  - Mail Merge Output Options
  - Producing Mail Merged Labels

- **Consolidation Exercises**

Producing A Mail Merge

What Is A Mail Merge?

A mail merge consists of two documents: a main document and a data source.

Mail merges are used when one document is to be sent to many people. For example, if you are a club or society with many members, you may wish to send all of the members a letter. Instead of manually typing the names and addresses into each letter, printing and sending, a mail merge can be produced.

All the names and addresses are held in one file (called a data source) and merged into the main document (the letter). The result is either a direct print of all letters to each member or a file containing all letters to all members.

The data source can be used over and over again so future mail-outs can be produced quickly and efficiently.

Common Uses of A Mail Merge

Standard letters

The most common document that is related to a mail merge would be the letter, where one letter is to be sent to many people. In most business situations the company or organisation would hold a database of clients or customers and would need to correspond with those people at regular times.

Producing a mail merge or mailshot is the obvious solution, it saves time and energy in inserting manually a name and address onto each letter.

Labels

Other types of document that can be produced using a mail merge facility include labels, which involve holding a data source, such as a database, table of names and addresses or other such information, then linking the label document with the data to produce a page of labels.

These can be address labels for parcels, name labels for a conference or meeting, visitor labels, or goods labels for boxes of stock for example.

Envelopes

Imagine having to produce (manually) 100 envelopes writing by hand on each one a complete name and address and the amount of time it would take! Mail merge can be used to link an instruction to produce envelopes using a data source of names and addresses to produce them en masse, instead of one by one.

Creating A Mail Merge

The first stage of the mail merge is to **create a main document** (such as a letter).

The letter would contain all standard information, leaving out the name and address of the recipient.

Save the main document in the normal way (**File**, **Save As**).

Click **Tools**, **Mail Merge** from the menu bar.

The **Mail Merge Helper** dialogue box is displayed (Fig 80).

There are 3 steps; the first step is to select what you want to create.

Choices include: Form Letters; Mailing Labels; Envelopes and Catalogues.

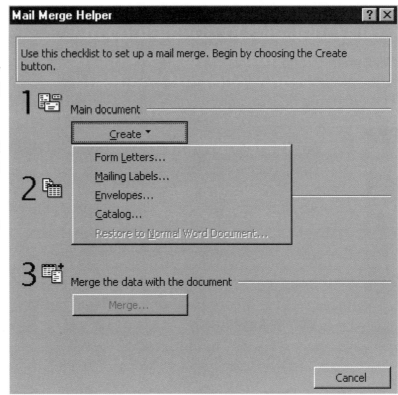

Fig 80

Select **Form Letters** to create a mail merge of a letter.

The following message will appear:

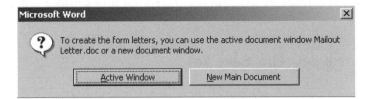

The mail merge can consist of an existing letter or a new document can be created.

If the letter to be used in the mail merge is already open, it will be in the **active window**. Click on this button to confirm.

The **file name** will now appear in the **Mail Merge Helper** dialogue box.

T A S K	
1.	*Open the document within the **Memoranda** folder called **Memo Building** for editing.*
2.	*Add the text '(See below)' after the text 'All Staff' in the 'To:' Section.*
3.	*Save the changes to the document.*
4.	*Using the Mail Merge Helper, complete **Step 1**, creating a form letter using the **Memo Building** document that you have open on screen (**active window**).*

Creating A Data Source

A data source is a set of data that contains information, normally about a particular subject or topic. For example, a set of data containing 'friends details'. The data source is made up of a series of rows (records). The rows are complete sets of data about one item, for example all data relating to one friend. Each row (record) is made up of fields with relevant field headings. A field is a single piece of data. Therefore a suitable field name for a data source containing 'friends details' would be 'Surname'.

Step 2 of the Helper requires the location of a data source.

If the data source exists, click **Open Data Source**.

If a new data source is to be created, click **Create Data Source**.

The **Create Data Source** dialogue box will be displayed (Fig 81).

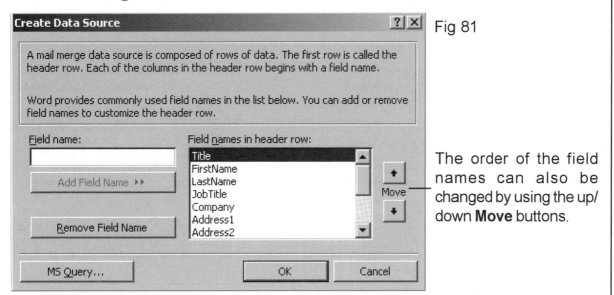

Fig 81

The order of the field names can also be changed by using the up/down **Move** buttons.

Field names are required to determine the type of data to be added to the mail merge. Field names appear along a header row (the first row) of the data source.

Field names can be added or removed using this dialogue box. For example, what information do you need to appear on the letter? When producing letters, you may require the recipient's Title, Full Name, Company Name and Address.

Not all field names will be required for your document. To remove unwanted field names, click to select them and click **Remove Field Name**.

To add a Field Name to the existing list (such as membership number or reference number), type the name in the **Field name** box and click **Add Field Name**.

When the list is complete, click **OK**. The **Save As** dialogue box will appear. Give the **Data Source** a relevant name. The data source will be saved as a file.

A message will then appear, informing you that there are no records contained in your data source (Fig 82).

Click **Edit Data Source** to enter the records.

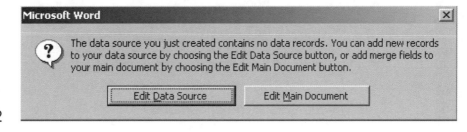

Fig 82

Fig 83

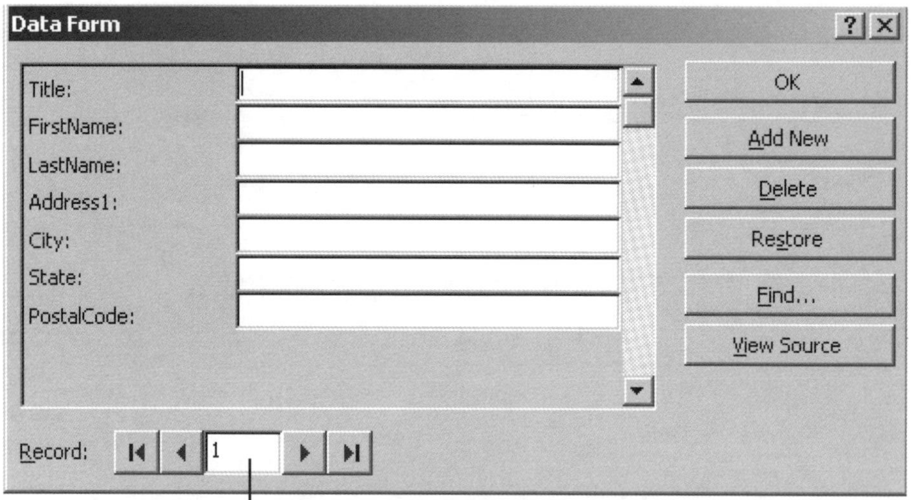

Data Form   [?] [X]

Title:		[▲]	OK
FirstName:			Add New
LastName:			Delete
Address1:			Restore
City:			
State:			Find...
PostalCode:		[▼]	View Source

Record: [◄◄] [◄] [1] [►] [►►]

Enter the records for each contact or company.

Notice the **Record** section at the bottom of the form. This will state how many records (people) are contained in your data source.

The **Data Form** will be displayed ready for data to be entered (Fig 83). The cursor will flash in the first box of the form. Each form represents one record (say for one person or one company). To move down the list to enter all information, use the **Tab** key on the keyboard.

When one record is complete, click **Add New**.

Once all records have been entered, click **OK**. The main document will now become active.

T A S K

1. Complete Step 2 of the mail merge by adding the following text as a data source. Save the data source as **Staff List** to your floppy disk:

FirstName	LastName	Department	JobTitle
John	O'Shea	Sales	Supervisor
Louise	Rogers	Sales	Personal Assistant
Jean	Wo	Training	Tutor
Angela	Howard	Marketing	Assistant Manager
Hema	Patel	Marketing	Supervisor
Jamie	Oldman	Marketing	Manager
Justin	Time	I.T.	Support Assistant
Kashira	Singh	I.T.	Support Assistant
April	Rogers	Sales	Manager
Kirsty	Smiley	Training	Tutor

2. Save the changes to the document.

Step 3 of the Mail Merge is to merge the data source (list of contacts) with the document (letter) to produce the same letter to multiple contacts at once.

To indicate where data will be placed on the document, the merge fields are inserted into place in the active document.

Move the cursor to the position of the first merge field (ie where you would like the address to appear).

The **Mail Merge** toolbar will now be displayed below the formatting toolbar.

Click **Insert Merge Field** and notice that the list of merge fields selected appears.

Click to select the first merge field (ie the Title) and press **Enter** to move to a new line. Click the next merge field and so on until all required merge fields appear in the main document.

The merge fields will appear similar to those in Fig 84 below. Notice that the FirstName and LastName fields were kept on the same line. **Add a space between the FirstName and LastName to separate them.**

The merge fields

Fig 84

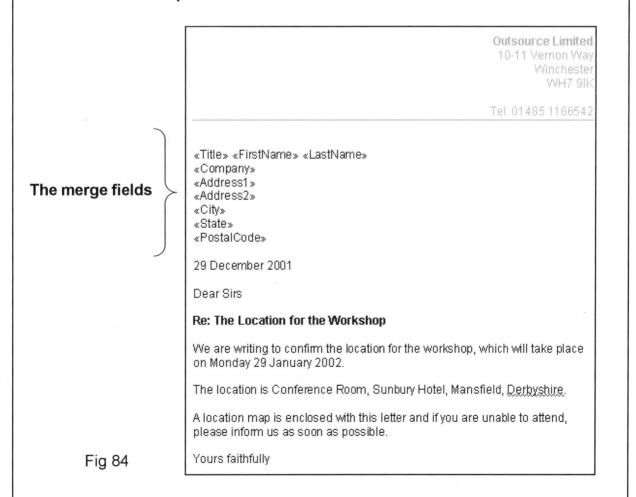

T A S K

1. *Move the cursor to the end of the memo (page 1), left align and change the font size to 12 pt.*

2. *Insert the merge fields as follows, leaving a space in between FirstName and LastName:*

    > FirstName LastName
    > Department
    > Job Title

3. *Ensure all merge fields fit on Page 1.*

4. *Save the changes to the document.*

Use the **ABC** button on the Mail Merge toolbar to view the data from the data source. Click again to view the merge fields. The button acts as an 'on' and 'off' switch. This is known as a 'toggle' button.

The final step is to merge the data with the document.

Click on the **Mail Merge** button on the toolbar. Merge... This will display the **Merge** dialogue box (Fig 85).

When merging to a new document, all letters will be contained in one document (ie if there are 5 records in your Data Source then the document will contain 5 letters).

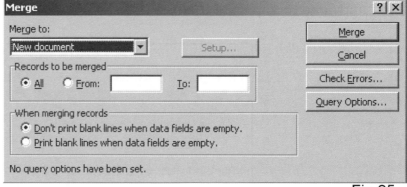

Fig 85

Click on the **Merge** button to create the mail merge.

Once the merge is complete, the merged document can be saved with a relevant filename.

T A S K

1. *View the data to ensure this is displayed correctly.*

2. *Merge all records to a new document and view the document.*

3. *Save the new document as **Staff Memo1** to the folder called **Memoranda**.*

4. *Close the document called **Staff Memo 1**.*

Previewing Merged Documents

You may want to preview the appearance of the merged documents. For example, you can preview the merged documents one at a time instead of merging all into a new document.

Ensure you are viewing the main document and click in **View Merged Data** on the Mail Merge toolbar.

This will display information from the first record in your data source in place of the merged fields.

To view information from other data records, click the arrow buttons on the **Mail Merge** toolbar, or type a record number in the **Go to Record** box and press **Enter** on the keyboard.

To print an individual record from this preview, click on the **Print** button on the toolbar. This will print the active merged document and not all merged documents.

T	1.	*View the merged data.*
A		
S	2.	*Navigate to records 3 and 5 and print both.*
K		
	3.	*Save the changes to the document and close.*

Mail Merge Output Options

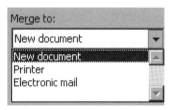

There are three options when producing an output for your merged documents: New document, Printer and Electronic mail.

New Document

The merged documents will appear in a new document and are separated from the main document. This is useful if the documents are to be saved (**Alt+Shift+N**).

Printer

The merged documents can be sent directly to the printer for an instant hard copy output (**Alt+Shift+M**).

Electronic Mail

If you have access to e-mail, and have included an e-mail address in your merge fields, this option will forward the document to all recipients via e-mail. The **Setup** button will become activated. Select the relevant merge field containing the e-mail address and enter a subject line. Click **OK** to send.

Producing Mail Merged Labels

A sheet of labels can be printed from any existing data source or a new data source using mail merge.

Open a new blank document and select **Tools**, **Mail Merge** from the menu bar.

Click on the **Create** button in **Step 1** of the **Mail Merge Helper** dialogue box and select **Mailing Labels**.

A message will appear (see right). Click on the active window to view the labels in the new document.

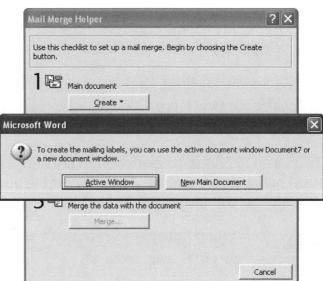

Move on to **Step 2** and select **Open Data Source**.

Select the **Data Source** file required. In this example **Staff List** has been selected.

Click on the button – **Set up Main Document**.

The **Label Options** dialogue box will appear - Word requires the size of the labels to use.

Select the correct size according to the labels you are using and click **OK**.

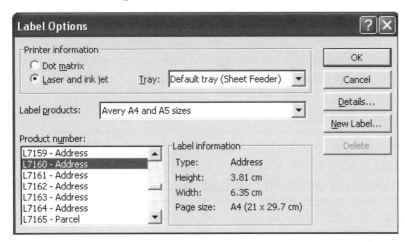

The **Create Labels** dialogue box will appear:

Click on the **Insert Merge Fi**eld to select the fields to appear on your label. Remember to place the fields side by side if they are related, for example **FirstName** and **LastName** will need to be placed together, separated by a space.

Click **OK** when they have all been selected.

Step 3 of the Mail Merge is to **Merge** the labels with the data.

Click on the **Merge** button.

The **Merge** Dialogue box will appear. Select the output required, such as to printer or main document, and click on **Merge**.

The labels will appear together with the data from the data source.

Save the labels document with an appropriate file name and print if required.

T A S K	1. *Using the data source **Staff List**, create address labels using the Mail Merge Helper.*
	2. *Use Avery A4 and A5 standard labels coded L7160 and save them to a separate new document called **Staff Labels**.*
	3. *Print the labels on plain paper. (The printer may revert to manual feed and may require user intervention, ie press the print feed button on the printer.)*

Problem	Solution
Creating a mail merge for a document other than a letter, label or envelope.	You can create a mail merge for any document in Word containing text and graphics, it does not have to be a letter. Select Form Letter and follow as per these instructions.
Creating a mail merge for a document in another version of Word.	You can use compatible Word documents such as: Word 2000, 97, 7, 6 and 2. As long as the main document is attached to a data source.
Changing mailing label size	Open the mail merge document and click on mail merge from the tools menu. Click on the Setup button under step 1. Amend the label specification to that required and re-insert the merge fields and merge.
When opening a document Word asks to locate the data source.	After selecting a data source for a main document, Word will look for this each time it is opened. If it is no longer used as a main document you can remove this link by clicking on Tools, Mail Merge, Main Document. Click on the Create button and select Restore to normal Word document.
Merge fields are printed instead of data	Turn off the display of field codes before printing. Tools, Options, Print (tab), clear the Field Codes check box. Click into main document and click Merge to Printer on the main merge toolbar.

CONSOLIDATION EXERCISE

1. Open the existing document **Outsource Report 2002** for editing.

2. Insert a page break below the paragraph headed 'New Staff' and ensure you are ready to insert text on page 2. Ensure that the spacing is single and that no indents have been applied. Format the text to Arial, 12pt.

3. Add the text below:

New Workshop Content

Psychology in the Workplace

This workshop will cover how different levels of Management handle the day-to-day running of an office. It will explore how the levels of communication can be improved simply by understanding colleagues' responsibilities. Most problems in the workplace are down to a lack of understanding & communication. This workshop will involve role-plays, discussion forums, brain storming sessions and question and answer sessions.

The power levels of management will be investigated, together with a discussion on how this affects employees with regard to motivation & enthusiasm.

A Guide to Good Management

This workshop explores the key features which make a good manager. The session will involve role-plays, question and answer sessions, scenario situations & an overall summary.

Those attending will be asked to fill out a questionnaire at the beginning of the workshop, answering some very blunt questions about their style of management at present! A follow up questionnaire is filled in at the end of the workshop and the two are compared. The results are then discussed in groups.

---

4. Use find and replace to replace the '&' symbol with the word 'and'. Replace the word 'blunt' with the word 'frank'.

5. Format the page and paragraph headings in the same style as the heading and sub-headings on page 1.

6. Format the text 'am' in the times, in the tabbed list to superscript.

7. Add the Company name **Outsource Limited** to the footer, aligned right. Add the © symbol.

8. Format the paragraphs on page 2 to double-line spacing. Save the changes, print and close.

CONSOLIDATION EXERCISE

1. Open the letter **L1OfficeMove** from the **Outsource Letters** folder for editing.

2. Position the cursor at the end of the letter (after the word 'Encs.') and insert a section break (next page).

3. Format page 2 (section 2) to have two equal-sized columns with a line between each.

4. Copy the Agenda from the document called **Outsource Report 2002** to column 1. Format the heading 'Agenda' to be centred, bold and 16 pt. (The copied text may need some adjustments to make it neat, ie remove hanging indents).

5. Insert a column break after the agenda items and type the following text into column 2:

   New Offices

   13-14 Vernon Way
   Winchester
   Lancashire
   WH7 9LK
   Tel: 01485 1166543

6. Centre the text in column 2 and make bold.

7. Save the changes to the letter.

8. Create a data source called **Outsource Staff** containing the following staff names and addresses to be used for a mail merge:

   Mr John O'Shea
   13 Bingham Road, Winchester, Lancashire, WH3 9IK
   Miss Louise Rogers
   44 Grove Alley, Winchester, Lancashire, WH3 8IK
   Mrs Jean Hunter
   56 Sycamore Avenue, Winchester, Lancashire, WH4 9YH

   Mrs Angela Howard
   56 Leaf Way, Winchester, Lancashire, WH10 6TG
   Mr Roger Mayhew
   98 Hilly Rise, Winchester, Lancashire, WH7 8YG

9. Insert the word fields as appropriate into the letter, positioned below the date.

10. Produce a print of the letter showing the merge fields. Print page 1 only.

11. Produce a print of the letter to Mrs Angela Howard.

12. Merge to a new document, view the document and save as **L1OfficeStaff**.

13. Close the documents, saving any changes.

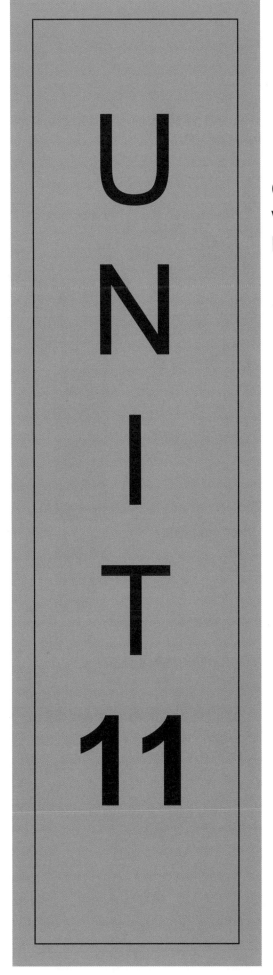

On completion of this unit, you will have learnt about and practised the following:

- **Working With Tables**

  - Creating A Table In A Document
  - Formatting Tables
  - Applying Shading To Tables
  - Inserting And Deleting Columns And Rows In A Table
  - Cell Alignment
  - Adjusting Row And Column Sizes
  - Splitting And Merging Cells In A Table

Working With Tables

Creating A Table In A Document

Inserting a table into your document will allow you to display information in a row and column format. Tables consist of cells which are individual boxes and can contain text and graphics. Fig 86 is an example of a table created in Microsoft Word 2000.

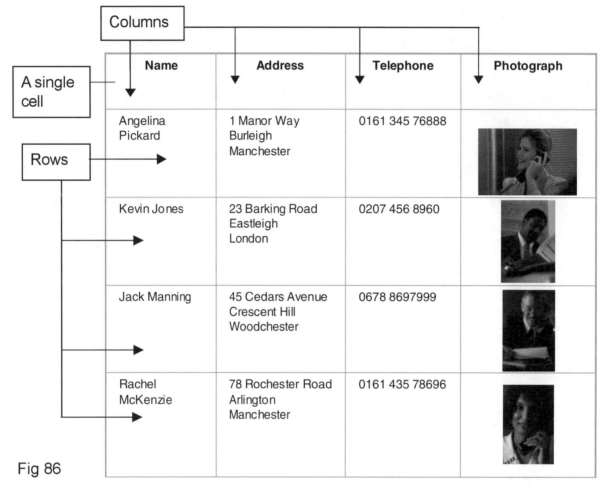

Columns

A single cell

Rows

Name	Address	Telephone	Photograph
Angelina Pickard	1 Manor Way Burleigh Manchester	0161 345 76888	
Kevin Jones	23 Barking Road Eastleigh London	0207 456 8960	
Jack Manning	45 Cedars Avenue Crescent Hill Woodchester	0678 8697999	
Rachel McKenzie	78 Rochester Road Arlington Manchester	0161 435 78696	

Fig 86

To insert a table, move the cursor to the required position within the document.

Fig 87

Click **Table**, **Insert Table** from the menu bar.

The **Insert Table** dialogue box (Fig 87) is displayed.

The number of rows and columns can be specified by either using the up and down arrows or by typing the number directly into the relevant boxes.

AutoFit behaviour allows you to determine a specified column width, choose to AutoFit to the contents of cells, or AutoFit to the window.

Click **OK** to create the new table.

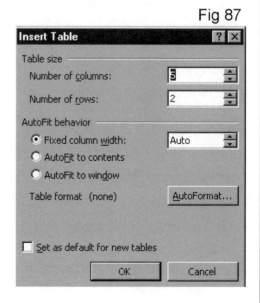

The table will be added to the document. To enter text into the table, click into a 'cell' and begin typing. To move between cells, use the **Tab** key on the keyboard or the arrow keys.

T A S K

1. *Open the document called **HSWorkshopPlan** for editing.*

2. *Insert a page break at the end of page 2. Insert the heading and table below on Page 3:*

Health and Safety Workshop Timetable

Date	Tutor	Location
3 April 2002	Stuart Riddings	Conference Room Building 3
6 April 2002	Jean Hunter	On Location - Safetech™
12 April 2002	Stuart Riddings	On Location - Safetech™
19 April 2002	Jean Hunter	Conference Room Building 1

3. *Adjust the column widths so that the text is displayed on one line by clicking in the table, select **Table** from the menu bar, click **AutoFit**, select **AutoFit to Contents**.*

4. *Format the heading of the table to the style called 'Custom Style' created on page 68.*

5. *Format the titles of each column (ie Date, Tutor and Location) to Arial, size 14pt, bold.*

6. *Save the changes to the document.*

7. *Print page 3 only.*

Formatting Tables

When inserting a table into a document, it will appear using single gridlines in black. To make the table stand out in appearance, it may be formatted. To format an existing table, select it by clicking anywhere inside the table. Click **Table**, **Select Table** from the menu bar. The table will now be highlighted.

Click **Format**, **Borders and Shading** from the menu bar and the **Borders and Shading** dialogue box (Fig 88) will appear. Ensure the **Borders** tab is displayed.

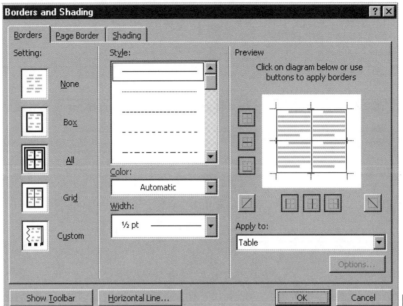

Fig 88

Formatting can be applied using the three sections **Settings**, **Style** and **Preview**.

The **Settings** section allows you to apply formatting to the outside edge of the table or to all lines in the table.

The **Style** section enables you to select a line style, colour and width.

The **Preview** section is a fast way of adding lines to sections of the table by clicking directly onto the grid.

Notice the **Apply to:** box displays 'Table'. Other options available are **Text**, **Paragraph** and **Cell**.

Once the formatting has been selected, click **OK** or click **Cancel** to abandon.

T A S K

1. *Format the table on page 3 to the following:*

   *Format **ALL** borders to a double-line style at 1½pts.*

2. *Save the changes to the document.*

Applying Shading To Tables

As well as applying a border line around any cell or range of cells in a table, you can apply shading too.

Select the column, row or cell(s) in the table.

Click on **Borders and Shading** from the **Format** Menu.

Ensure the **Shading** tab is selected.

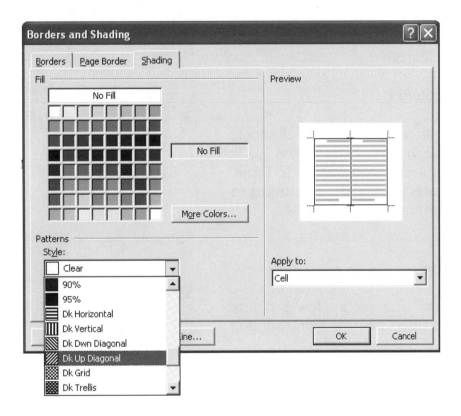

The **Shading** dialogue box is similar to the **Borders and Shading** box for text, only the **Apply to** box states 'Cell' to indicate that a cell or range of cells in a table have been selected.

The **Fill** section will allow you to select a different fill colour for the cell(s).

The **Style** section will allow you to select a different shade of grey or a pattern for the selected cell(s).

The **Preview** section will display the updated changes you have made in this dialogue box.

Inserting And Deleting Columns And Rows In A Table

Once a table has been created, information may need to be added at a later date. However, this may not have been catered for when creating the table initially. Word 2000 has the facility to edit existing tables to allow you to add individual data in cells, remove data to leave a blank cell or remove entire columns and rows. Once deleted, existing rows and columns will readjust themselves to suit the table.

Inserting a row

The new row can be inserted above or below the location of the cursor in the table. Position the cursor in the row required and click **Table, Insert, Rows Above** or **Rows Below** from the menu bar (Fig 89).

Inserting a column

The new column can appear to the left or right of the selected column when inserted. Click into the column required and click **Table, Insert, Columns to the Left** or **Columns to the Right** from the menu bar (Fig 89).

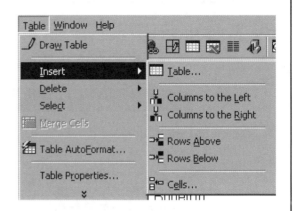

Fig 89

Deleting a row

To delete a row, click into the row and click **Table, Delete Rows** from the menu bar (Fig 90).

Deleting a column

To delete a column, click into the column and click **Table, Delete Columns** from the menu bar (Fig 90).

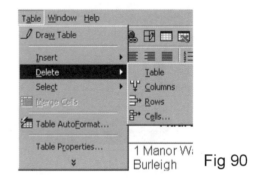

Fig 90

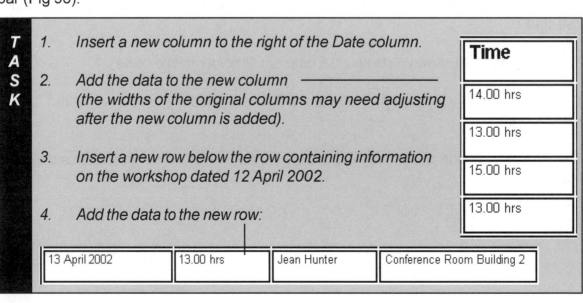

T A S K

1. Insert a new column to the right of the Date column.

2. Add the data to the new column ———————— (the widths of the original columns may need adjusting after the new column is added).

3. Insert a new row below the row containing information on the workshop dated 12 April 2002.

4. Add the data to the new row:

Time
14.00 hrs
13.00 hrs
15.00 hrs
13.00 hrs

13 April 2002	13.00 hrs	Jean Hunter	Conference Room Building 2

Cell Alignment

Data contained within a cell in a table can be formatted to enhance the appearance of the overall table. For example, certain data such as dates or times may look better right aligned within a cell.

You can work with individual cells or a selection of cells when formatting.

- To work with a single cell, click into the cell.

- To work with a selection of cells, highlight the range of cells.

- Alternatively, highlight a column or row of cells.

When the selected cell or cell range has been highlighted, position the mouse pointer over the highlighted cell(s) and click on the right mouse button.

This will display a sub-menu of options for use with the cells (Fig 91).

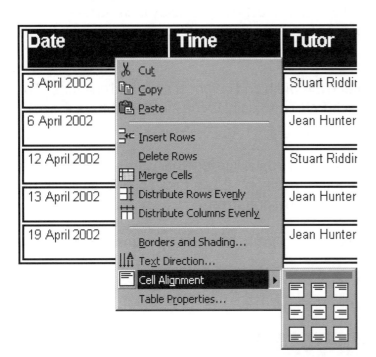

Point to (do not click on) **Cell Alignment** to display the alignment options.

Options include:

Align Top Left (default)
Align Top Centre
Align Top Right
Align Centre Left
Align Centre
Align Centre Right
Align Bottom Left
Align Bottom Centre
Align Bottom Right

Fig 91

T	*1.*	*Align the column titles to Centre.*
A		
S	*2.*	*Align the dates and times appearing in the table to Centre Right.*
K		
	3.	*Save the changes to the document.*
	4.	*Print page 3 only.*
	5.	*Close the document.*

Adjusting Row And Column Sizes

When working with tables, it may be necessary at times to adjust the height of a row or cell and the width of a column or cell.

In this example of a table (below), column widths and row heights have been amended:

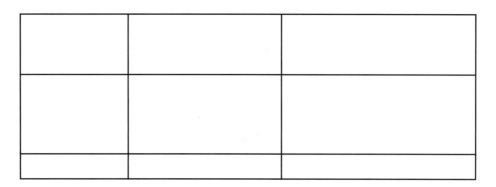

As you type into the cell, the cell height will adjust to the contents by increasing in size to adjust to the text being typed in. In some cases, a more consistent row and column height is required.

There are two methods in which to amend the width and height of rows and columns. The quickest way (however, not the most accurate) is to point to the join lines where the rows and columns meet.

The mouse pointer will change to a vertical or horizontal line together with two small arrows. Click and hold this and drag to the required position. It can take some practice to get perfectly correct results, so use the next method if preferred.

Select the **Row** or **Column** required and click on **Table**, **Table Properties** from the menu bar.

The **Table Properties** dialogue box will appear. Ensure the **Column** tab is selected.

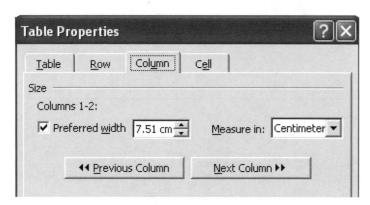

You can specify a preferred width by putting a check in the box and using the up and down arrows to select a new measurement, or type in your own.

Other columns can be sized from here without having to reselect them. Click on either **Next Column** or **Previous Column** and size as required.

To specify the Row height click onto the **Row** tab.

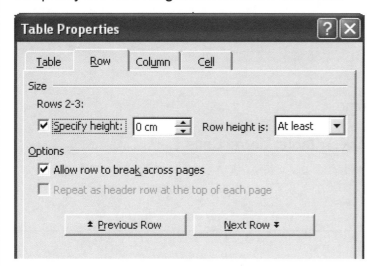

Again, put a check in the box to specify the height and either use the arrows or type in a measurement.

Insert other measurements as required for other rows by clicking on the **Previous Row** and **Next Row** buttons.

Splitting And Merging Cells In A Table

Once a table is drawn or created in Word, you are not restricted to the layout of cells that you have selected.

You may decide, for example, that you require 5 rows and 4 columns and create the table in this manner, then find that you have not allowed for a title heading within the table.

You can achieve this by merging cells together to create one cell across the table, as shown below:

This is the Merge set of cells			
These	Are	The	Table
Of	cells		

The above table was created by selecting 4 columns and 5 rows.

To merge the first row of cells into one, select the row required.

Click on **Table**, **Merge Cells**.

The cells will now appear as one.

The same can be achieved for a column.

Select the column(s) required and click on **Table**, **Merge Cells**.

Here is an example:

The above table was created with 3 columns and 3 rows; the third column has been merged to appear as one whole cell.

The opposite of merging can be achieved - that is, splitting the cells in columns and rows.

You may have a table like the example below:

This table contains 3 columns and 2 rows.

To split the top left cell into two, click into the cell.

Select **Table**, **Split Cells** from the menu bar.

Insert the number of columns to split the cell into and the number of rows if required.

Click **OK**.

The result will appear as shown above.

T A S K

1. Create a new blank document.

2. Create the following invoice document using a table:

Invoice Number:			Fix It Designs Limited		
To:			1020 The Strand		
			Carpingham		
			London		
			CP45 8HY		
			Tel: 09786 395996		
			Fax: 09786 395997		
			Date:		
Qty	Details		Rate	Unit	Total
	Additional Instructions:				
	Create an initial table containing 22 rows and 5 columns.				
	Use Arial Font for all text.				
	Allow 14 rows for the Invoice details.				
	Row Height 1cm				
Registered Office: 2 Park Lane, Withingham, London, W1 7TG					

3. Save the document with the name **Fix It Invoice**.

4. Print the document. Save any changes and close the document.

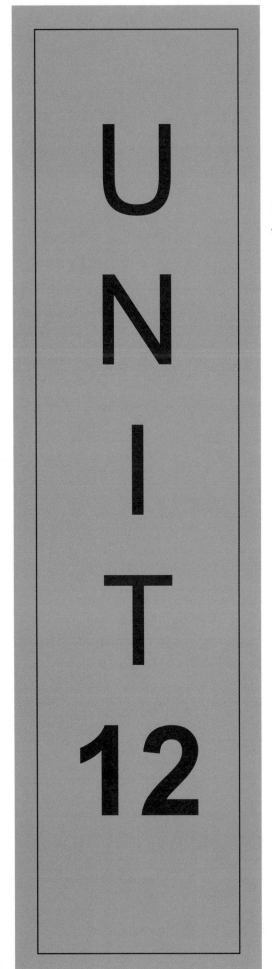

On completion of this unit, you will have learnt about and practised the following:

- **Producing Drawn Objects**

  - The Drawing Toolbar
  - Formatting Drawn Objects
  - Fill Effects
  - Adding Text To Drawn Objects
  - Working With Layers
  - Grouping
  - Grouping And Layering Multiple Objects

Producing Drawn Objects

The Drawing Toolbar

Word 2000 has a facility to produce objects in documents which have been drawn. This can be particularly useful when producing company logos or for drawing objects such as box shapes, lines and arrows.

To produce the objects, use the drawing toolbar (Fig 92). If this is not showing, click on the **Drawing** button on the toolbar.

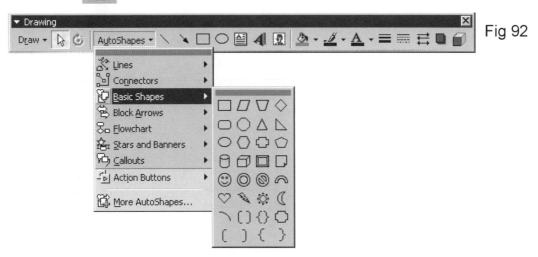

Fig 92

Producing a company logo using the drawing toolbar

1. Click on the shape required from those available on the drawing toolbar.

2. Move the mouse pointer to a location within your document and click. Drag and release the left mouse button to draw the shape.

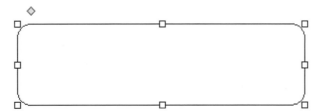

3. The shape will appear, together with 'selection handles'. The selection handles are used to resize the shape to make it larger or smaller, longer or shorter. This depends on which selection handle is used. To resize the shape, click and hold a handle and drag to position.

T A S K

1. *Start a new blank document.*

2. *A logo is required for use on the Charity Sports Day. Select the Hexagon AutoShape and draw the shape to a suitable size.*

Formatting Drawn Objects

Once the shape has been drawn in a document, it can be formatted to include a 'fill' colour, line colour and a line style.

To work with any object in Word 2000 the object must be selected, ie click on the object to select it (the selection handles will appear).

To format an object, click to select it, select **Format**, **AutoShape** from the menu bar and the **Format AutoShape** dialogue box will appear (Fig 93).

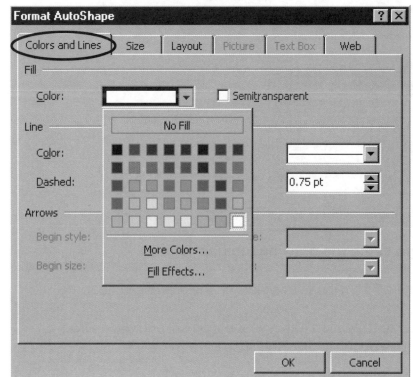

Ensure the **Colors and Lines** tab is selected.

To change the **Fill** colour of an object, click on the drop-down arrow and click to select an alternative colour.

Use the remaining **Line** drop-down boxes to change any line style or colours as required.

Click **OK** to confirm.

Fig 93

Fill Effects

A drawn object can be formatted to appear in a different colour to stand out in a document and it can also be filled with fill effects and patterns.

To apply this, click on the drawn object to select it:

Select **Format**, **AutoShape** from the Menu bar.

The **Format AutoShape** dialogue box will appear.

Click on the drop-down menu in the **Fill** box. Click on **Fill Effects** to reveal more fill options.

Select the **Pattern** tab to reveal the **Pattern** options:

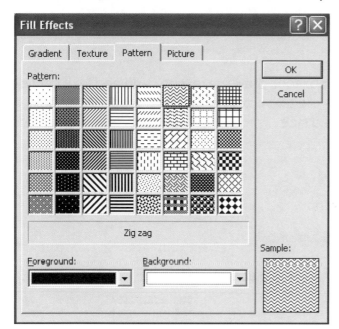

A grid of patterns will be displayed. Click on each pattern to preview a sample at the bottom right corner.

You can change the foreground and the background of an AutoShape or Drawn Object by using the drop-down menus at the bottom of the dialogue box.

Click **OK** to confirm your selection.

Your shape will appear patterned.

T A S K

1. *Format the hexagon to have a fill colour of Light Blue.*

2. *Format the hexagon to have a black line border, 1½pt in thickness.*

3. *Save the document as **Charity Logo**.*

Adding Text To Drawn Objects

The **Drawing** toolbar has a tool called '**Text Box**'. This will enable you to add text to any shape.

To draw a text box, either click on the text box tool, draw the text box and add text, or click on the text box tool and click once where the text box is to be positioned. When text is inserted, the box will expand to the required size.

To add text to a document:

1.   Click on the text box tool.

3.   Click once in a blank area of your document.

4.   There will be a flashing cursor indicating the place you may begin to type.

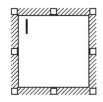

5.   Type the text and format the text in the same way as normal text, ie use the formatting toolbar or **Format**, **Font**. Text can also be aligned inside the shape. Use the alignment buttons on the toolbar.

My Company Logo

To format the text box, either with a fill colour or to change the line colour or remove the line, select it and click **Format**, **Text box** from the menu bar.

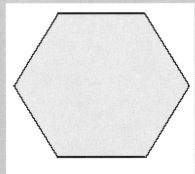

T A S K

1.   *Add a text box to the document.*

2.   *Insert the text 'Outsource Charity Sports Day'.*

3.   *Format the text to be Tahoma, size 14pt, bold and centred.*

4.   *Format the text box and remove the black line border and fill colour.*

5.   *Save the changes to the document.*

Outsource Charity Sports Day

Working With Layers

When adding objects to a document, they are automatically 'Layered' - for example:

Notice that the Star is behind the Smiley Face and this is behind the Arrow; they are in **layers**.

To change the order of an object, first select the object and then use the **Drawing** toolbar.

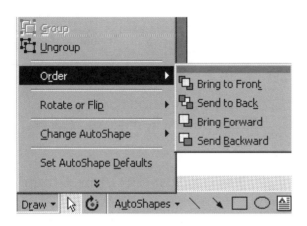

To send the Arrow to the back of the Smiley Face, select it and click on **Draw**, **Order**, **Send Backward**.

The Arrow will now appear like this:

T **A** **S** **K**	1.	*Place the text box on top of the hexagon AutoShape as a layer.*
	2.	*Save the changes to the document.*

Outsource Charity Sports Day

Grouping

When working with drawn objects, each object acts as an individual. In some instances, working with the objects one by one is not practical, therefore the 'Group' feature is used.

Grouping objects together has the added benefit of being able to format objects all at once instead of individually.

To group a selection of objects, use one of the following methods:

- Click **Edit**, **Select All** from the menu bar (this is recommended if all objects in the document are to be grouped together).

- Use the **Select Objects** tool on the drawing toolbar. This will allow you to draw a box around the objects you require grouping.

- Click on each object in turn (being careful not to drag), whilst holding down the **Shift** key on the keyboard. If you add a component by mistake, click on the object once more to de-select it.

Once all drawn objects are selected, from the Drawing toolbar click **Draw**, **Group**.

You will notice that the objects have now become one object and a new set of selection handles will appear. The objects can now be copied, moved or inserted as a file into another document or application.

To ungroup the object, select it and click **Draw**, **Ungroup** from the drawing toolbar.

T A S K	1.	*Use the **Select Objects** tool to group together the text box and the hexagon AutoShape. Move the grouped object to the top left corner of the document.*
	2.	*Save the changes to the document.*
	3.	*Print the document.*
	4.	*Close the document.*

Grouping And Layering Multiple Objects

As previously discussed, grouping means to select more than one object in a document and group them together to become one. Layering objects changes the order in which objects appear in a document.

Multiple objects can include drawn objects, AutoShapes, lines, arrows, text boxes, charts and graphs and graphics.

In the example below several objects have been created in a Word document:

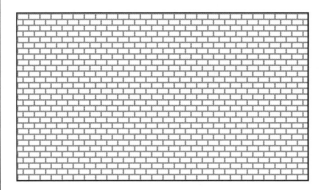

The objects consist of a text box, an auto shape and a drawn object (rectangle).

The first step is to layer the object to appear as required.

The rectangle is to appear at the very back of all objects.

The star is to appear in front of the rectangle but behind the text box.

To achieve this, click on the star object to select it and drag to place in the position, ie top left corner of the rectangle. On release of the mouse the object will be positioned.

Ensure the star appears in front of the rectangle in a layer. If this does not appear, send the rectangle to the back.

The second step is to reposition the text box in the bottom right corner of the rectangle.

Again, if this does not appear in front of the rectangle, send the rectangle to the back using the order command.

The completed object should appear as shown below:

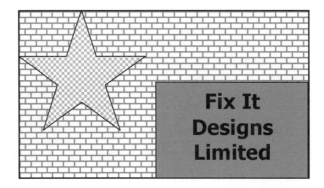

All objects are still separate drawing objects and can be selected individually. This means that if the objects needed to be repositioned they would all have to be moved separately.

By grouping the objects together the whole logo can be moved as one.

To group the objects, click on each object whilst holding down the **Shift** key on the keyboard.

Select **Draw**, **Group** from the **Drawing** toolbar.

The object will now appear as one object and can be moved accordingly.

To edit the individual objects at any times, select **Draw**, **Ungroup** from the menu bar. The objects will appear as separate objects.

T A S K

1. *Create the logo as shown below, group it and create layers as shown.*

2. *Save the document with the name 'logo' to your floppy disk.*

3. *Print the logo.*

4. *Save the changes to the document and close.*

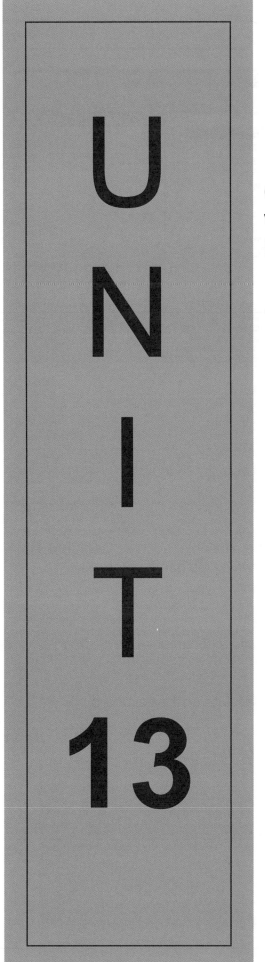

On completion of this unit, you will have learnt about and practised the following:

- **Inserting Objects**

    - Inserting Fields
    - Inserting Documents
    - Inserting Charts And Graphs
    - Inserting Graphics
    - Resizing Inserted Objects

Inserting Objects

Inserting Fields

Fields are used to insert specific information relating to your document. They have a code behind them and, instead of having to type in a code to get a result in the document, you can use **Insert**, **Field** from the menu bar.

This will display the **Field** dialogue box (Fig 94).

For example, instead of typing in the date and time, a field can be inserted into the document to automatically display this.

Fig 94

To insert a field into a document, click **Insert**, **Field** from the menu bar.

The dialogue box is split into sections:

Click on a category name to display the field name available, such as **Date and Time**, **Date** field. Notice that a description will appear when a field name is selected.

To insert the field, click **OK**.

To view any field codes which have been inserted into a document, use the 'toggle' keys **Alt + F9** on the keyboard to show and hide them.

To delete any field codes, highlight them and press **Delete** on the keyboard.

TASK

1. *Start a new document.*

2. *Type in the text below:*

Health and Safety Report 2002

Safetech™ has compiled this report for Outsource Limited.

This report covers the hazards found in Buildings 1-3 between June 2001 and December 2001.

A Risk Assessment has been carried out in each building to identify potential hazards in the workplace. A total of 15 hazardous areas were found, the most serious being listed below:

Building 3 fire escape blocked by stationery boxes
Building 2 fire escape locked
Building 1 fire escape stairway blocked by a damaged desk
Trailing cables found in Building 3 Marketing department
Exposed electrical cables found in the entrance to Building 2

It has been recommended by Safetech™ that the Company enrols a member of staff in each building to be a Safety Representative. The staff selected would be responsible for keeping a safe environment for all employees. They will hold monthly meetings regarding safety. Problem areas can be identified and an action plan put into place.

The key to working in a safe environment is to enlist all members of staff into safe thinking. They should be made aware that it is every individual's responsibility for their own safety.

Staff should be prompted to report any potential hazard to their Safety Representative immediately.

---

3. *Format the heading of the document to a suitable style.*

4. *Format the list of hazards found to a bulleted list.*

5. *Fully justify all paragraphs and ensure all text (apart from the heading) is Arial, size 12pt.*

6. *Save the document as **HSReport2002**.*

7. *Position the cursor at the end of the document and insert the following Fields: **Filename**; **Savedate**.*

8. *Ensure the document fits to one page, check the document for spelling and grammar, print the document, save the changes and close.*

Inserting Documents

A Word document can be inserted into another Word document. This method can be used when one document is to be created from several separate documents, perhaps created by different people.

Before inserting a file or document, have the active document open, into which the other document will be inserted. If necessary, insert a **Section** or **Page Break**. This is used when the file to be inserted is of a different format, (ie columns or tables).

Click **Insert**, **File** from the menu bar (Fig 95).

The **Insert File** dialogue box will appear. This is similar to the **Open** dialogue box.

Locate the file required and click **Insert**.

The file will appear in the document, merged with existing data.

Fig 95

Resave the document or save the new merged document with a new name.

T A S K

1. Open the document called **Meeting** for editing.

2. Insert a next page section break below the text on page 3.

3. Ensure you are ready to insert text on page 4 and set the page layout for this section only to landscape. Ensure that indents are removed, spacing is set to single and before and after is set to 0.

4. Set the margins for this section only to:

   Top & Bottom: 3 cm   Right & Left: 2.5 cm

5. Insert the file (document) called **Workshop Schedule**.

6. Make minor adjustments as necessary if the formatting has altered in any form.

7. Print preview the document.

8. Save the changes to the document.

9. Print page 4 only.

Inserting Charts And Graphs

A chart or graph is a graphical representation showing the relationship between quantities.

Charts and graphs are mainly produced in Microsoft Excel. However, they can be inserted into a Word document.

The chart or graph will appear as an object in a document, together with selection handles for resizing.

To insert a chart, click **Insert**, **Picture**, **Chart** (Fig 96).

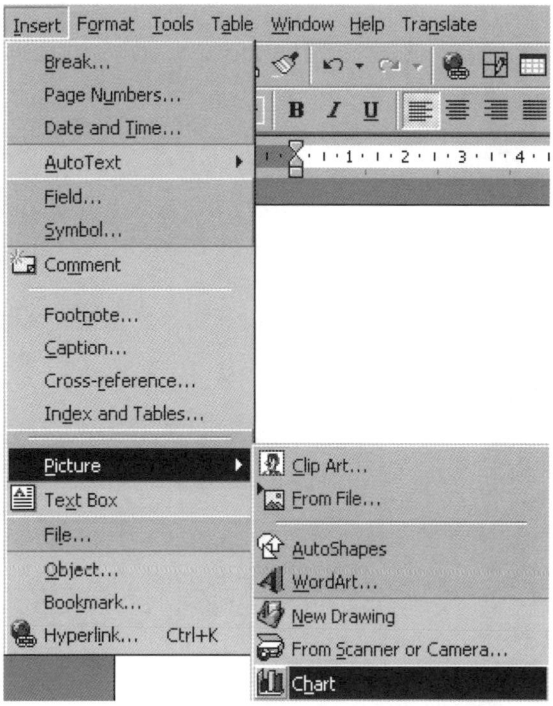

Fig 96

A sample chart will appear, containing sample data (Fig 97).

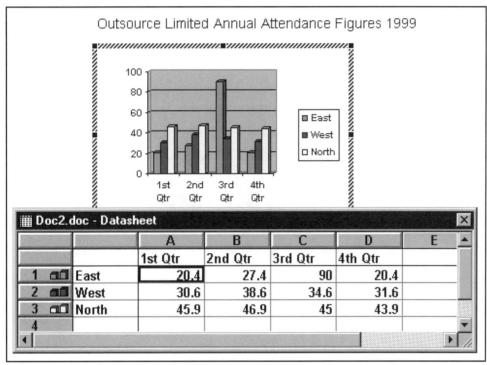

Fig 97

The datasheet consists of columns and rows. The columns are headed alphabetically and the rows are headed numerically. They act similarly to grid references. Each box containing data is called a 'cell'.

To produce a chart, click into a cell and type over the existing data appearing in the datasheet. To delete unwanted remaining data, click into the cell and press the **Delete** button on the keyboard.

1. Open the document called **HSReport 2002**.

2. Insert a page break at the bottom of page 1.

3. At the top of page 2, type in the heading **Risk Results** and format to a suitable style from those available.

4. Insert a chart to contain the following data below the 'Risk Results' heading.

HSReport 2002.doc - Datasheet		A	B	C	D	E
		Jan-May	Jun-Dec	Jan-May	Jun-Dec	
1	Building 1	3.00%	50%	25%	90%	
2	Building 2	10%	40%	25%	50%	
3	Building 3	40%	30%	60%	10%	
4						

Once all data has been entered into the datasheet, click on the cross at the top right of the datasheet box to close it. The chart in the background will have been updated to display the current data (Fig 98).

Use the selection handles to resize the chart as necessary.

Click anywhere outside of the chart to deselect it.

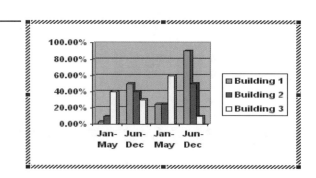

Fig 98

1. Close the datasheet and move the chart so that it is positioned under the heading.

2. Print preview the document.

3. Save the changes to the document.

4. Print page 2 of the document and close.

Inserting Graphics

Inserting Clip Art

Microsoft Word has a built-in feature called the 'Clip Art Gallery', which is a library of images. To make a document more powerful, images can be inserted which relate to the type of document being created, such as business images for a document relating to a Company report or letter.

To view the Microsoft Clip Art Gallery from within a document, select **Insert**, **Picture**, **Clip Art** from the menu bar or use the Clip Art icon on the drawing toolbar.

Once an image has been inserted, it can be resized and moved to suit the document.

To display the Clip Art Gallery, click **Insert**, **Picture**, **Clip Art**.

A list of Clip Art categories is available (Fig 98).

To view images, click on the Category name.

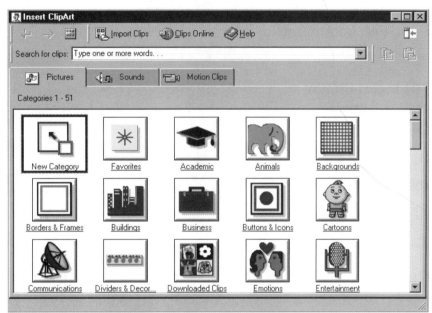

Fig 98

Click on an image to insert it and then select the **Insert** button from the menu (Fig 99).

The Clip Art Gallery will remain open.

Click on the **close** button when all required images have been inserted.

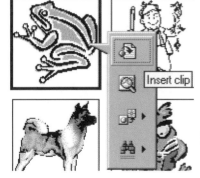

Fig 99

T A S K

1. Open a new document.

2. Insert an image of your choice from the available Clip Art images.

3. Close the Clip Art Gallery. Close the document without saving the changes.

Inserting an image from disk

Having explored Clip Art and the Clip Art Gallery, there are other options when inserting images or Clip Art into a document. An image or piece of Clip Art can be saved to disk, such as the floppy disk, as a file. There are other storage locations in which a piece of Clip Art can be obtained, such as a CD-ROM.

There are many CD-ROMs available, containing thousands of images. The Internet is also a useful resource for obtaining images, depending on the copyright implications.

To insert an image from floppy disk:

Click **Insert**, **Picture**, **From File**, from the menu bar (Fig 100).

The **Insert Picture** dialogue box will be displayed:

Change the location to read **3½ Floppy (A:)**.

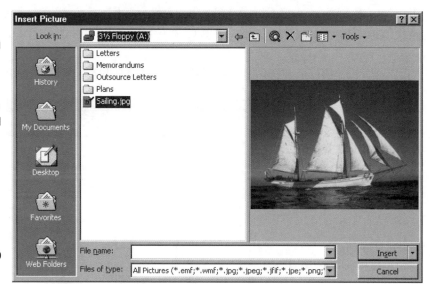

Fig 100

Select the image file required. A preview of the image may appear on the right, allowing you to view the image before inserting. If a preview does not appear, click on the **Views** button and select the **Preview** option.

Click Insert and the image will appear in the document. Use the move handle or selection handles to reposition the image if required.

Image files are available in various formats. The format will dictate the resolution, quality and size of the graphic. To view the type of image file and its size, view the contents of the disk in Windows Explorer.

.bmp   Bitmap image, available in a variety of formats, can display millions of colours.

.gif   Graphics Interchange Format, used on the World Wide Web, displays compressed image formats and are therefore smaller file sizes. This format can also be animated (moving pictures).

.jpeg or .jpg Joint Photographic Experts Group, commonly used on the Web, is used for displaying high quality photographic images, containing many colours.

Resizing Inserted Objects

All objects, when selected appear with selection handles. Selection handles are small black squares that appear all around an object. They are used to resize objects.

↕	Extend the box vertically
↔	Extend the box horizontally
↘	Extend the box diagonally to the left*
↗	Extend the box diagonally to the right*
✛	Reposition or move the box on the page

*Depending on which selection handle is selected.

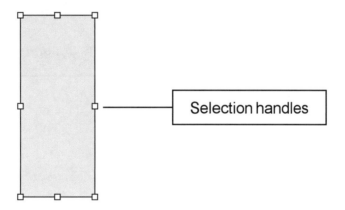

Selection handles

To resize the object, rest the mouse over any selection handle, and click and hold with the left mouse button. Drag to the required size or shape and release the mouse button.

You may wish (especially when resizing image and chart objects) to keep the object in proportion. This means that if you have a photo in a document, when it is resized it will retain its aspect ratio and not appear distorted or stretched.

There are a number of options in order to achieve this:

To resize a selected object	Hold down
Proportionally from a corner	**Shift** and drag a corner sizing handle
Vertically, horizontally or diagonally from the centre outward	**Ctrl** and drag a sizing handle
Proportionally from the centre outward	**Ctrl+Shift** and drag a corner sizing handle
While temporarily overriding the settings for the grid	**Alt** and drag a sizing handle

TASK

1. Open the document called **Memo Sports** for editing.

2. Insert a suitable image from the Clip Art Gallery.

3. Position the image below the existing text and centre the image on the page (to centre the image, select it and click on the **Centre** button on the toolbar).

4. Save the changes to the document.

5. Print the document.

6. Close the document.

7. Open a new blank document.

8. Insert the picture from your floppy disk called **Sailing**.

9. Save the document as **Sailing** and close the document.

CONSOLIDATION EXERCISE

1. *You have been asked by your supervisor to construct a questionnaire to be used at a new workshop, 'A Guide to Good Management'. Sketch a suitable layout for the questionnaire and include all information below. Leave sufficient space for the answers to the questions. Use a table layout, refer to the example overleaf if necessary.*

Include:

Company name with copyright symbol
Header - Questionnaire
Name of Workshop
Name of Tutor

Questions:

1. On a scale of 1-10, how effective do you think your Team members are?
2. Do you feel in control of your Team members? If not, why not?
3. Do you feel that your Team is producing the results required?
4. What improvements (if any) do you think are required in your Team?
5. Do you feel respected by your Team members? If not, why not?

2. *Add a box at the bottom of the questionnaire for any comments.*

3. *Insert your name as a footer.*

4. *Insert a next page section break.*

5. *Save the document as **Workshop Questionnaire**.*

6. *Open a new document and design a company logo, use an AutoShape from those available. Use a fill colour. Use the text **Outsource Limited** and format the text as appropriate. Group the text and the shape to become one object.*

7. *Save the document as **Outsource Logo** and close.*

8. *Insert the document **Outsource Logo** into the document **Workshop Questionnaire**. Place the logo at the top of the questionnaire. Resize if necessary.*

9. *Insert the document **Outsource Report 2002** at the end of the questionnaire and save the merged document as **Outsource Report 2002 V1**.*

10. *Insert the fields, date, time and file name at the end of the document and save any changes. Print and close.*

Example Questionnaire

QUESTIONNAIRE

Name of Workshop	A Guide to Good Management
Name of Tutor	Stuart Riddings

1.	On a scale of 1-10, how effective do you think your team members are?

2.	Do you feel in control of your team members? If not, why not?

3.	Do you feel that your team is producing the results required?

4.	What improvements (if any) do you think are required in your team?

5.	Do you feel respected by your team members? If not, why not?

Comments:

EXERCISE

1. *Now that you have learnt much more about layout, presentation and formatting, amend the sketch that was produced in the task on page 12 of this workbook, applying the skills learnt.*

2. *Open the word processing package and produce the flyer.*

3. *Save the flyer as a template with the name **Workshop Flyer**.*

4. *Print the template.*

5. *Close the template.*

APPENDIX 1

The Microsoft Word 2000 Window

Definition of Terms

The Standard Toolbar

The Formatting Toolbar

The Microsoft Word 2000 Window

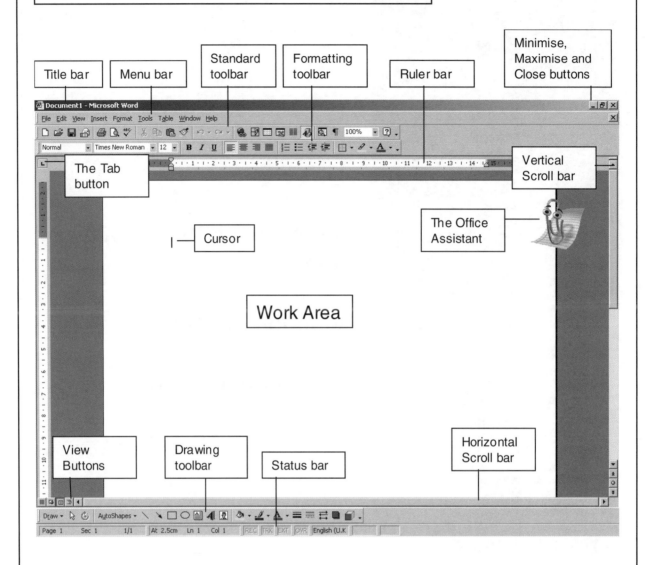

Title bar

Menu bar

Standard toolbar

Formatting toolbar

Ruler bar

Minimise, Maximise and Close buttons

The Tab button

Vertical Scroll bar

Cursor

The Office Assistant

Work Area

View Buttons

Drawing toolbar

Status bar

Horizontal Scroll bar

Definition of Terms

Title bar	Displays the application name and the name of the active document. The Minimise, Maximise and Close button for the application appear on the right side of the title bar.
Menu bar	Each menu item displays a drop down list of further commands.
Standard and formatting toolbar	Bars containing buttons; each button represents a command.
Cursor	A blinking vertical line in the work area, often known as the 'insertion point'. The cursor will indicate the position at which text will be inserted.
Minimise	A function used to hide the document or application from view.
Maximise/ restore	A function used to make the application or document full screen or partial screen (a toggle command).
Close	Closes the application or the active document.
Status bar	The status bar displays information regarding the active document such as the current page and section number, the line and column positions.
Work area	The input area for text entry and editing.
Scroll bars	Scroll bars are used for navigating through your document.

The Standard Toolbar

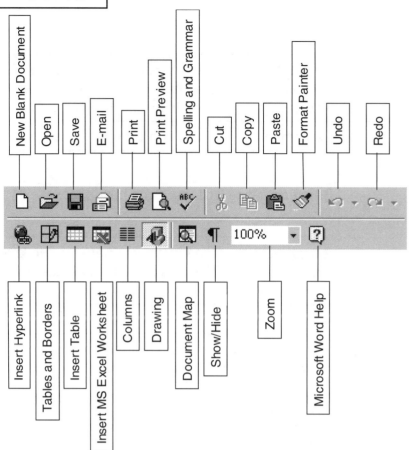

The Formatting Toolbar

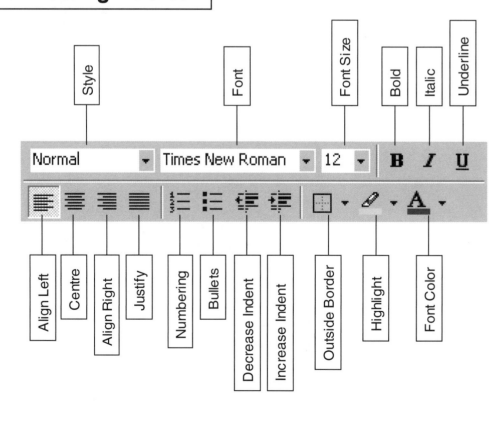

APPENDIX 2

Microsoft Word 2000 Help

Microsoft Word 2000 Help

Help!

How to use the help function

Microsoft has an excellent system to help when you perhaps cannot remember how to do something, or you are unsure what an item or subject is referring to. Microsoft displays help in different ways, with or without an Office Assistant.

The following explanations and screens display help without an Office Assistant.

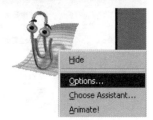

Office Assistant

Click **Help**, **Microsoft Word Help.**

If the Office Assistant appears right-click on the assistant and select **Options**. In the resulting dialogue box, click in the box

to remove the tick in the **Use the Office Assistant**. Click **OK**. This removes the Office Assistant from your screen.

Click **Help**, **Microsoft Word Help** to display the help screens.

Help toolbar

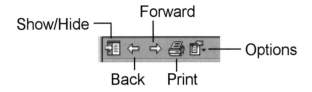

Show/Hide - Shows or hides the left pane so that once a search has been completed the search criteria can be hidden to display just the results.

Go **Back** - moves the view backwards through previously selected search criteria.

Go **Forward** - moves the view forward through the previously selected series of search criteria.

Print - allows you to print the topic.

Options - gives a further selection of choices.

Left Pane   Right Pane

Click on the **Contents** tab.

Click on the book symbols to open the subjects. Click the question mark to read the information on the subject shown in the right hand pane. Click on the book symbol to close the subject.

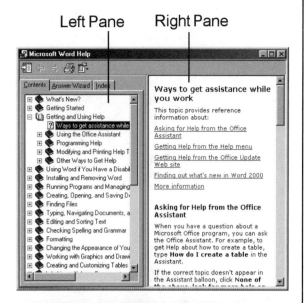

Click on the **Answer Wizard** tab.

Type in a keyword that you wish to find. Click **Search**. Select the topic from the list on the left-hand side and the result will appear in the right-hand pane. The search can be further defined by selecting the topic from the right pane by clicking on it.

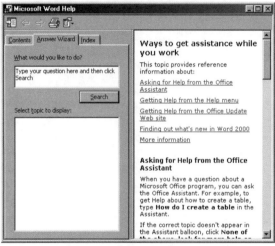

Click on the **Index** tab.

Type in a keyword that you wish to find or select a topic from the scrolling lists in **Choose keywords** or **Choose a topic**. Click **Search**. The results of your search will appear in the right-hand pane.

APPENDIX 3

Word Glossary

Word Glossary 1

Application	Software program which carries out a specific activity such as word processing, spreadsheets or databases.
AutoText	A stored item (text or graphical) which can be used repetitively.
Bullet	A small mark, usually square (but can be customised) which is used to add emphasis to lists.
Click	To press and release the mouse button.
Clipboard	A standard Windows feature which allows you to temporarily store text or graphics which can then be pasted into documents.
Command	An instruction issued to the computer to carry out a certain action.
Current folder	The folder into which the document will be saved, unless specified otherwise.
Cursor	The small flashing vertical line which appears on screen. This identifies the point at which text will be entered.
Cut	To remove a section of text or graphic from the current document and place it on the clipboard.
Default setting	A value, action or setting that is automatically used when no alternate instructions are given.
Dialogue box	A window that displays the options available for your chosen command.
Drag	The process of clicking the mouse button, keeping your finger pressed down and moving the mouse at the same time.
Ellipsis	A punctuation mark (…) consisting of three dots. Menu items or command buttons with an ellipsis will open a dialogue box.
File extensions	All Windows applications automatically append their own file extensions as follows: Word .doc Excel .xls Access .mdb
File formats	The application under which a file was originally created will determine its format. Different file formats may not necessarily be read by other applications, unless they are able to convert them.

Word Glossary 2

File name	The name given to an individual document.
Folder	The storage place for your documents. You can name folders in just the same way that you would name folders on your desk or in your filing cabinet.
Font	Also referred to as typeface. The appearance of your printed characters, eg Arial or Times New Roman.
Footer	A piece of text or graphic which is automatically placed at the bottom of every page.
Format	A general term which relates to the display of text in a document.
Frame	A box inserted into a document into which you can place text or graphics.
Formatting toolbar	Displays buttons you can click on to perform common editing tasks and apply text enhancements to documents.
Function keys	A set of keys usually labelled F1 through to F12 and located on the top row of your keyboard. Pre-programmed in some applications to provide shortcuts.
Global template	All new documents created in Word are based on a template. Unless specified otherwise, the template used is Normal.dot.
Header	A piece of text or graphic which is automatically placed at the top of each page.
Highlight	To select a piece of text or graphic for changing. The highlighted section usually appears as black.
I-Beam	The I-shaped mouse pointer which you move over the text.
Indent	To offset text from the margin, usually used to emphasise a particular paragraph.
Insertion point	May be referred to as cursor. The flashing vertical bar in the active document indicating where text will be inserted or deleted.
Landscape	Orientation of the paper where the longer edge is to the top.
List box	A drop-down menu from which you choose an option.
Macro	A shortcut for recording a series of commands or keystrokes, storing them in the computer memory.

Word Glossary 3

Memory	The storage areas, temporary or permanent, for computers or printers.
Menu	A drop-down list of options available from which to give commands.
Merge	To combine data from a main document to that of a data list using the mail merge facility.
Message box	Window which appears either giving information or warnings related to the command being carried out.
Mouse button(s)	A mouse generally has two or three buttons. Commonly, the left button is used to operate the program and the right mouse button can offer shortcuts for the user.
Mouse pointer	Mouse pointers change, depending on the activity and the position on screen. Different points include: I-Beam, hourglass, single arrow, double arrow, question-pointer and four-directional pointer.
Movement keys	Located to the right of the main keyboard and used to control movement of the insertion point within a document.
Non-proportionally-Spaced Font	A typeface which gives each character exactly the same amount of space, regardless of how much space it actually requires.
Page Break	The point where one page ends and another begins.
Paste	To insert items from the Clipboard into a document. These can be textual or graphical.
Point Size	A unit of measurement used to indicate font sizes, ie 12 or 14. One point equals 1/72 of an inch.
Print Preview	The facility to view on screen how the document will appear when printed.
Proportionally-spaced font	A proportional font allocates each character exactly the amount of space it requires.
Protected space	A special instruction given to prevent words being split when word wrap occurs.
Ruler	A part of the screen used for controlling margins, indents and setting tab stop points.
Select	To click on a file, folder, graphic, text box or select any other area of text.

Word Glossary 4

Shortcut key	A keystroke or combination of keystrokes that offer quick access to a Word feature.
Sizing handle	The small solid squares that appear around the border of a graphics box when it has been selected. Used for resizing or moving an object.
Subscript	Text that appears slightly lower and smaller than surrounding text, eg H_2O
Superscript	Text that appears slightly higher and smaller than surrounding text, eg 2^x.
Tab	Horizontal points along the document used for aligning text.
Template	Special documents that create a basic outline on which to base further documents.
Text box	A box into which can be placed text or graphics, which can then easily be moved throughout the document.
Word wrap	The process whereby a word processing package moves text on to the next line when it is unable to accommodate any more on the current line.
Wizard	A feature that asks questions and then used the responses given to create a specific type of document.
WYSIWYG	'What you see is what you get' - the facility to immediately see the impact your formatting has on the document, prior to printing.